PYTHON PROGRAMMING FOR BEGINNERS

2 Books in 1

The Ultimate Step-by-Step Guide To Learn Python Programming Quickly with Practical Exercises

D1464478

© Copyright 2022 - All rights reserved.

TABLE OF CONTENTS

other languages. Let's briefly explore reasons to learn Python with a list. Lists are easy to digest and remember.

- User-friendly: Programming languages allow communication between humans and machines. Python is a high-level programming language, which means it is closer to human language than machine language. Machines do not understand Python on their own. There is an interpreter that translates Python code into machine language.

- Powerful: Despite how easy it is to learn, Python is immensely powerful. It is just as useful as languages like C++, which are low-level programming languages. Places like Google, Microsoft, IBM, Xerox, and NASA use Python. You can even use Python to develop games.

- OOP: Object orientated programming is one the most effective programming paradigms. It allows programmers to treat problems, actions, and data like real-world objects represented in code. It is not always best to use it, though, which makes Python interesting because it is a multi-paradigm language. This means you can use it for object-orientated programming, functional programming, and others. It's flexible. You can benefit from OOP while using techniques belonging to other paradigms.

- Computer-friendly: Python doesn't require a lot of processing power or RAM to run. For instance, developers use Python to create little robots that are operated by $5 computers. It can also run on any operating system. It means you can develop your application on different operating systems simultaneously, and it will still work the same. It also means your programs will be able to run on multiple platforms.

- Language adaptability: You can combine Python with other languages to take advantage of the different features and advantages. For instance, you can combine it with C++ to take advantage of the system optimizations and speed it offers in the backend.

- It's free: Python is free and open-source. The license allows you to make changes to the source code in a way that fits your purposes. At this point, this might not be important to you, but it might be later on.

- Community: There is a huge Python community online. This is because Python is open source, has broad applicability, and is easy to learn. So, you will find many people dedicated to learning or teaching the language. And if you get stuck, you will find help easily. You will find plenty of collaboration opportunities with other people on the same path as you as well.

Installing Python

Before we get started, you will need to download and install Python on your system. The installation procedure is very easy. It is just like the installation of any other program on your system.

To do so, go to www.python.org and go to the "Downloads" section. Once you get there, pick the right installer for your system. Make sure you are downloading the latest version as well.

When the installer has downloaded, run it and follow the steps. Do not change anything.

We advise that you install Python and get used to working on it on your system. Online platforms are good for practice, but not for building things. So, working on your system will help prepare you better. We also advise that you write the code yourself. If you copy and paste, experiment with the code. Doing this will help drill the lessons in you.

Using a Text Editor

You can write Python in almost any text editor. There are many to choose from. There are programs like Notepad, Notepad++, gedit, and others. Some text editors will be better than others as they provide features that are useful to programmers. For instance, Notepad++ has syntax highlighting, meaning you will be able to see when you make errors in your code and fix them. Other editors like Notepad are plain, meaning you will not be able to tell you are making a mistake until you try running the code. Try picking a text editor that feels natural to you.

Avoid using word processors.

Using an IDE

An IDE, Integrated Development Environment, is a program for writing code that comes with multiple important features for programming. Many come with graphical interfaces, have autocomplete, history functions, and are integrated with other debugging tools, can run commands, deploy, and more. The advantage of using an IDE is convenience. IDE's have many support features, shortcuts, reminders, and suggestions on how to fix errors.

One of the most popular IDE's is IDLE. IDLE comes with Python. IDLE can run in two modes: interactive and script. Interactive is best when you want Python to respond immediately to your code.

There are many IDE's out there. Do a little research and pick the one you like best.

Your First Program

Now that you are set up, it's time to write your first program. We will be using IDLE for this example, but you can use a text editor or an online Python console if you like. We recommend you use IDLE so you familiarize yourself with IDEs.

Run IDLE in interactive mode. It is easy to find. Just search for it on your system and click on it. The window you will see is called a Python shell. There will be a blinking cursor, indicating you can type. Type the following:

3. **The computer system**: Then, you need to anticipate the operating system of your audience. Are they going to be on a Windows, Apple, or Linux computer? Sometimes you will need to think about the device they are more likely to use. Is it an Apple tablet or an Android phone? You don't have to be too specific. You need to have an idea so you can make some provisions for it while you code.

All of these questions will guide the design of your applications. When you answer them at the beginning of a project, you make the road ahead a lot simpler. If you don't have answers to all these questions for some reason, it is fine. Some of the answers will come to you as you develop.

Finding the Solution

You now have a basic idea of what you want to build, where it works, who it is for, and how it must work. It might look like you don't need to carry on any longer thinking about it, but there is still work to do. Many developers spend a lot of time designing their programs instead of actually coding. Now you need to ask yourself what your intended target's requirements are. Then understand their needs. It might involve an agreement between you and the client if you are building this for someone specific. Once you understand what they want, you need to think about a solution. The solution might not be obvious, it might be tenuous, and it might get complicated. Still, if you have written down your process, you will have an easier time adjusting your strategy and avoiding other issues. You also save yourself a lot of time. There is no point building it only to discover you have to start over and change it because no one wants it. Here are some things to think about at this point:

- Functional requirements: These are the things that your program has to do. Your program's functional request is what the system has to do to give you the result you want. For instance, it might need to calculate and print a message or the answer. You cross these steps off as you code.

- Results: When the time comes, you will need to test your program to see if it behaves as it should. When you start, it will be fine running the application to see if it does what you want it to. As you mature and your applications become more complex, you will need to find better testing methods. Testing skills help reduce bugs and ensure good performance. In some cases, you might write some tests that have predetermined answers and see if the program delivers the answers you expect. You will do this during the development stage, not after you have finished. It's daunting having to go back over the rest of your application to figure out why it does not work. It is time-consuming and will be testing. As a beginner, it will be enough to just run your program and see that it works.

- Maintenance: When you design a program, you need to think about how it will be used. Software meant to be used often needs maintenance and support. This means you need to have plans for changes, updates, and extensions. But if your program is web-based you need to find ways to update it without taking it down. To make maintenance easy, you need a program that is easy to read. You'll find that most developers do this the entire lifetime of their software. Software needs to adapt with changes and improve to stay relevant.

All this requires your code to be clear and reusable. It is the simple things which will make upgrades and maintenance easy to do.

Below is an example of a software design document of the "Hello World" program we built:

Problem: The system needs to display a message to the user.

User: Me

Operating System: Windows / Linux

Interface: Command line terminal

Functional requirements: Print a line of text

Testing: Perform application run test, making sure text is displayed.

Start Designing

Now you are ready to start designing the application. You do so by writing the program in pseudocode, which you can later translate into code. Pseudocode uses English to describe what a program should do at each stage to deliver the results we want. Pseudocode explains every line of code or block of code that we should write, the inputs it should receive, how it acts, and what it should output. Also, pseudocode allows you to brainstorm. For instance, you start envisioning the data types, variables, and functions you will need to make the applications work.

There are no specific rules to pseudocode. You can write it any way you want. This only changes when you work with other programmers because you will have to use the standard chosen by them. In most contexts, pseudocode follows the syntax and rules of other languages, but the functions and commands are written in words, not in code. But right now, there is no need to talk about this as you don't know the language. What you need to understand now is the idea behind the structure. Here's how you write pseudocode:

```
# Start program
# Enter two values, X and Y
# Add the values together
# Print sum
# End program
```

All pseudocode is commented out so that Python ignores it when you run it. If you don't comment it out, you will get errors. The example above shows us the main design of your program. It's a description of all the code necessary for the program to achieve its goal. When you fulfill each one of these, the program will execute.

16

Improving Your Pseudo Code

Readability remains an important factor when writing pseudocode. Python interprets spaces and tabs as delimiters, and they are interpreted in different ways, affecting how the app behaves. In your pseudocode, you can use indentation to indicate which logical statements and actions go together, but because you commented out the pseudocode, your indentation will not affect the code. It means you can use whichever kind you feel comfortable with. We will discuss this more in upcoming chapters.

The first line of a code block is always written without indentation. All the code that belongs to it is indented into subsections. If you write your pseudocode in a way that resembles Python code, writing the needed code will be easier. It is why developers advise pseudocode be written this way. For now, write the pseudocode in a way that makes sense to you. As you learn the syntax, you will use the Python code structure. Below is the pseudocode following the same principles:

```
# Perform the first task
# Enter the first value
# Verify whether the value is text
# Print the value
```

It makes things clear, and the developer knows where to place the code. To create a separation between this code block and another, you only need to put an empty line between them and begin the next block without indentation. Now, you can write out your design following these principles.

Summary

In this chapter, we looked at the software design cycle. We saw how the process of creating a Python program starts. We learned how to break our problems into objectives and tasks. We also learned about the role pseudocode plays in the development and Python's pseudocode principles. This chapter emphasized the importance of planning and outlining your applications to avoid problems further down the road. Now that you know all this, you are ready to learn the language itself.

CHAPTER 3:

Variables and Data Types

Variables are like containers used to store data values so the computer can process them. Without variables, the processes would not occur because there would be nothing to process. Data values come in different types: lists, integers, strings, floats, dictionaries, and more. In programming, many functions rely on the use of variables for their functionality. Variables allow us to write operations without knowing the exact data the function will manipulate. In fact, computers convert most kinds of data into variables.

In this chapter, we learn about variables and data types. We will see the fundamental role played by variables in the development of any program. We will learn with real examples where we will manipulate strings and perform mathematical operations.

Python Identifiers

When coding, you need to be able to identify a data type by its label. Identifiers are labels/words that are not commented out or placed within quotation marks. Identifiers label things so the code is more readable, provided that the names relate to your project. Don't use the same identifiers for multiple variables or functions; conflicts will occur. So, your identifiers have to be unique to each variable.

Identifiers allow you to use any word you want except those reserved by Python. Those used by Python are an integral part of the language, and they are known as keywords. Some of those keywords are: False, lambda, class, import, global, while, yield, continue. You will come to understand these later as you learn. Because you won't always remember these keywords, Python warns you when you use one.

Now, let's learn how to name variables. Variables should always start with an underscore or a letter. This is not a rule; you can break it, and your programs will run. It is a convention established by other programmers for a good reason. You can use numbers in your variables as long as your identifier does not start with one. Also, Python is case sensitive, meaning the following name variable would not count as the same variable: "newVariable," "NewVariable," "NEWVARIABLE," and "_newVariable." Python will see each one as a unique variable, although semantically, they are the same. It means you should watch your capitalization. Experienced developers advise you to stick to one style throughout your project. So, if you start your variables with an uppercase letter, you should follow the same rule in your entire project. It prevents unnecessary confusion between you and other programmers.

Introduction to Variables

Defining, declaring, or introducing a variable is done in two stages. You will find this is true in most programming languages. The first stage is an initialization, where a container is created with the appropriate identifier. The second stage is an assignment where a value is placed in the container. Both are performed in one operation. Here's an example of it below.

```
variable = value
```

You perform the initialization and define assignment through the equals sign.

A block of code that does something is called a statement. The assignment is the statement. Expressions are code that evaluates to obtain a value/result. Below is a list of assignments, and at the end, we have an expression that gets the total price.

```
number = 0
product_weight = 2.1
price_per_kilogram = 10
filename = 'file.txt'
trace = False
sentence = "this is an example"
total_price = product_weight * price_per_kilogram
```

In programming, you need to be orderly. You should write every statement in a line. In the example above, we have a list of assignments similar to a grocery list. When writing a program like this, you need variables that you can use to perform various tasks. For now, understand that variables come in different types, and these types make up a program. They serve as ingredients to a recipe. Before we start exploring the types, let's discuss dynamic typing in Python.

Python and Dynamic Typing

In Python, the data type of a variable is automatically inferred, which means you don't have to specify it when you write code. This is called dynamic typing. Most programming languages want you to specify whether your variable is a number, list, or dictionary. Dynamic typing allows us to be less verbose. It allows us to focus more on functionality.

The disadvantage of this is that Python will not warn you when you make certain mistakes,

19

like adding variables that we shouldn't add together. Python will assume that is what you mean to do. Beginners face the tricky task of keeping track of their variables: where they are assigned, what their values are, and how they change. One tip to doing this is declaring your variables at the top of a code block. This way, they are all at the same place where you can easily inspect them, allowing you to easily follow your code. The other tip is creating a design document. You can also create a table where you will declare all your variables. Knowing and keeping track of your variables will enable you to troubleshoot and maintain your code with ease.

Dynamic typing allows Python to flag variables used with the wrong data type. So if you perform an operation using both, your operation will be invalid, meaning you receive a "TypeError," like the one below:

```
x = 2
y = 'text'
trace = False
x + y Traceback (most recent call last):
File "<stdin>", line 1, in <module>
TypeError: unsupported operand type(s) for +: 'int' and 'str'
y - trace Traceback (most recent call last):
File "<stdin>", line 1, in <module>
TypeError: unsupported operand type(s) for -: 'str' and 'bool'
```

You don't have to understand the code to appreciate what just happened. The x variable is a number, and the y variable is text. You can't perform calculations with words and numbers. That is why you get an error. You can add words together to form sentences or even add sentences together. You can also do mathematical operations with numbers. What you can't do is mix both. This TypeError is called the Traceback. It tells you to go back and fix something in the logic of your program. This is an example of many other TypeErrors Python will warn you about. You need to ensure the operations you want to perform don't break real-world rules about how they should work.

In the previous example, we have two types of variables: an integer (int) and a string (str). Strings are text or words, and integers are whole numbers. These are some of Python's data types. Python provides ways of combining variable types to form more complex data types; we will explore this later. For now, let's build our programming foundations by practice.

Basic Text Operations

Strings are a popular data type in any programming language. We used one when we made our "Hello World" program. In that program, we used one print statement. So how do you print multiple statements? If you use the methods we used without the first program, you just add another print statement in the next line. There are other ways of doing this, like concatenation. Concatenation is combining strings into one. You can perform concatenation in several ways. Below, it is done by separating variables by a comma:

```
characterClass = "warrior"
characterGender = "male"
print (character gender, characterClass)
The output will be "male warrior."
```

You can also use the strings themselves instead of the variables that hold them:

```
print ("male" "warrior")
```

The output will be "malewarrior." When using this method, you need to add space, so the output has space between the words. You can add an extra space at the end of the first word or the beginning of the second. Here's how you'd do it:

```
print ("male " "warrior")
or like this:
print ("male" " warrior")
```

The output will be "male warrior."However, concatenating strings in this way may cause problems. Here's one below:

```
print (characterGender "warrior")
The result will look something like this:
File "<stdin>", line 1
print (characterGender "warrior")
∧ SyntaxError: invalid syntax
```

You'll get an error like the one shown above when you attempt concatenating strings to a variable in this way. You can only do this with two separate strings.

You can use the plus operator to combine strings. In Python and most programming languages, it is referred to as a concatenation operator because it combines strings. Here's how it looks:

```
x = "male"
y = "warrior"
x + y
The output will be "malewarrior."
```

Python also uses the plus symbol to do mathematical operations. So concatenating strings this way requires Python to assess the variables first, meaning it works harder. So don't use this method unnecessarily, as heavy usage will cause the program to demand more from the system. This is an example of design planning. When you concatenate many strings, try to find other methods and only use them when you don't see a better alternative.

Quotes

In Python, quotes are important. You might have already seen this as we were going through the previous examples. Quotes mark characters and words as text. A character is defined as a single letter, punctuation mark, number, or space. A text is really a string of characters. This is why the data type is called "string." Python separates text from commands and keywords using quotes enclosures. So far, we have only used double quotation marks, but Python offers other ways of doing this.

For instance, you can write the "Hello World" program with single or double-quotes. Here's how you would do it:

```
print ("Hello World")
print ('Hello World')
```

Both of these will produce the same results because Python will not see a difference between the two. So you will have to choose whichever you prefer. Then how do you test a block of text that has multiple lines? Python allows you to use block quotes with all their breaks and spaces. Here is how you would do that:

```
x = '''    this is a long line of text
    that requires multiple lines'''
y ="""" this is another long line of strings
    but this time, we're using double quotes
    because they're cooler """
```

Both methods will produce the same results, albeit using single or double quotation marks. Python will read them the same, so it all comes down to what you prefer.

Now, how do you use quotes inside a string? To do this, you have to use different quotation marks. For example, double quotations for the string and singles quotes for what is quoted. Like this:

```
x = "She told me to 'quote' like this"
```

In the example above, we have a quote hierarchy, where double quotes make the string and the single quotes mark the quoted text. In singles quotes, we have a substring, and in double-quotes, we have the main string. This is called a nested quote.

Developing a Text Application

We now know a bit about software design, texts, and strings. Let's put all that to practice. We are going to create a script that generates information about characters in a roleplaying game. We will name variables for name, gender, race, and description. All of them will be strings. Python will print the output on the display.

You have the knowledge you need to do all of this. Before you follow the example below, try developing your own program. Here's our example:

```
"""""
myFile.py
```

Problem: Generate information on roleplaying characters

Target audience: Personal / Friends and family

System: Windows / Linux

Interface: Command Line

Functional requirements: Print a character sheet.

Users will input name, gender, race, and description.

Test: Basic execute test.

```
"""
Name = ""
Gender = ""
Race = ""
Description = ""
# Prompt user for information
Name = input ('what is your name? ')
Gender = input ('what gender are you? (male / female / not
sure): ')
Race = input ('what race are you? (Human / Elf / Orc / Dwarf /
Gnome): ')
# Output character sheet
cool_line = '<__==|#|==--++**\$/**++--==|#|==__>
print("\n", cool_line)
print("\t", Name)
print("\t", Race, Gender)
print("\t", Description)
print(cool_line, "\n")
```

If you closely, this is the improved version of our Hello World program. We used the same techniques to create something a bit more complex. First, we have our design document that provides information about the program. Then we made use of escape sequences in our code: "\t" for "tab" and "\n" for "newline." Escape sequences are used to format text, making it easier to read. Whitespaces are one of the typical ways text is formatted, and this is why these two are used often.

We have a character sheet. Now it is time to come up with an attribute for them. We can do that through numbers.

Numbers

Numbers are assigned to variables the same way you would assign strings or any data type. Here's an example:

```
x = 5
y = 2
```

Python will be able to discern whether it is dealing with a number because of the absence of quotations or letters. In this instance, an integer. Before we go any further, you need a basic understanding of how computers work.

Computers store data in binary, a sequence of ones and zeroes. Information is processed by triggering a vast amount of switches that can either be on or off (1 or 0). There is much more to learn about this topic, but this is enough information for our purposes.

Let's look at some numeral types:

- Integers: In programming and mathematics, whole numbers are called integers. Integers don't have decimal points, but they can be negative or positive. Integers are frequently used in operations.

- Floats: Floats have decimal points. If 2 is an integer, 2.5 is a float. Floats can also either be negative or positive, and they are assigned to variables the same way integers are. Python can differentiate between floats and integers automatically.

- Booleans: They are the most basic type there is, and they represent how computers work. A Boolean can either be True(1) or False(0). They are often used with logical operators like "and", "or" and "not." We'll explore this in detail later. Variables are assigned Boolean values using True and False keywords. They are always capitalized; otherwise, it will not work.

Basic Operations

You have seen how we assign values to variables. We will now perform some basic operations like add (+), subtract (-), multiply (*), and divide (/). When you perform operations like these, you create an expression. Expressions are code that the computer has to work through to get a result. Expressions can be assigned to variables. Below is an example:

```
strength = 10 + 2
dexterity = 10 - 4
endurance = 6 * 2
awesomeness = strength + dexterity * endurance
awesomeness
84
```

You are probably surprised to find the result isn't 216. It isn't, because Python understands math, so it knows which calculations have precedence over which. The calculation is like this: (10 + 2) + ((10 - 4) * (6 * 2)).

This example shows how Python evaluates expressions and decides which sections go with which. There are many more operations in Python. To fully understand the kind of process that occurs when these decisions are made, you need to know Python has operator precedence. This tells Python which operator to pay attention to first. If you don't want Python to use its default, you can guide it, like below:

```
awesomeness = (strength + dexterity) * endurance
```

Now the result is 216 because it has to start with the expression in parentheses.

We have only worked with integers, but the same rules would still apply even if we used floats.

Python also lets you convert numeral types to other numeral types. Here are the most common ones:

1. Converting any number to an integer: int (x)

2. Converting any number to any float: float (x)

3. Converting any value to a string: str (object)

Note how our focus is now functions instead of operators. The syntax change makes this obvious. We are manipulating values contained in parentheses. Parentheses are part of the function. Here are some examples below:

```
float (12)
12.0
int (10.4)
10
float (int (15.5))
15
```

Now that we have explored numerical data, let's create an application to apply everything we have learned.

Developing a Number Application

One of the most important things to learn before you start building more complex programs is storing data and comparing values. In other words, you need to learn about conditional statements and data manipulations of other data types. Before you do so, you need to understand how to manipulate numerical data types.

Say you want to buy material to make curtains from. You need to know what material you need and how much of it will be enough. You calculate this based on the size of your windows. Your functional requirements are the window dimensions, which you will use to determine how much material you need to buy, and its cost. Then you do some research. As a programmer, you'll need to research topics you know little about. In this case, you will investigate how much curtain material is calculated. Alternatively, you can go to a fabric store and talk to experts. Once the research is completed, you can make your software design document. Make this a habit. You will be happy that you did. Here's how it would look:

```
# Prompt user to input window dimensions measured in centimeters
# Consider a margin of error and add to the dimensions
# Calculate the width of the fabric
# and calculate the length of the material for one curtain
# You need two curtains, double the quantity of material
# and divide by 10 to have the dimensions in meters
# Calculate the price of everything
```

`result`

ormation about the width of the material and price per meter. A width of 150
urrency units per meter. We would need to get information about the height
he windows. This data will be given to us by the user, meaning we will use the
input function. The function will give us a string, which we will need to convert into a float.
Then we can make our calculations: Here's how it should look:

```
# One roll of material is 150 cm in width
# One meter of material costs 10 units of currency
material_width = 150
price_meter = 10
# Prompt the user to input the window measurements in cm
window_height = input('What is the height of your window (cm):
')
window_width = input('What is the width of your window (cm): ')
# Extra material is needed for the hems
# Convert the string to a float
# Without the conversion you will not be able to do the math
curtain_width = float(window_width) * 0.75 + 20
curtain_length = float(window_height) + 15
# Calculate how much material you need
# The calculation is done in widths
# Calculate the total length of material needed for every
curtain (stick to cm)
widths_of_cloth = curtain_width / material_width
total_length = curtain_length * widths_of_cloth
# Double the quantity of material because we have two curtains
# Remember to divide by ten in order to calculate meters
total_length = (total_length * 2) / 10
# Calculate the price
price = total_length * price_meter
# Print the result
print("You require", total_length, "meters of cloth for ",
price)
```

Please note that the numbers in this example aren't accurate because we did not use actual
information about curtains and fabric. Only when we do can we offer the correct result. For
our purposes here, this does not matter; we have learned a lot regardless.

Summary

We learned about variables and assigning values to them. We explored basic data types like
integers, floats, and strings, and performed text and numerical operations. With strings, we
learned how to combine them and convert them. You have enough knowledge to create a
basic program that takes input and outputs results based on those inputs. It's very basic, but
these are the foundations you need to build more complex applications. In the next chapter,
we learn how to teach programs to compare values and make decisions.

CHAPTER 4:

Decision Making in Python

You have learned how to design applications and manipulate numbers and strings. Now, you need to learn how to add more functionality to your applications. The more you learn there, the more complex your designs will become, too, because you will be dealing with complex problems. Remember to always visit your old applications as you learn. Update and improve them. This is one of the most typical roles a programmer has to perform. Also, the exercises help you gauge your progress.

In this chapter, we will learn several methods that will allow us to compare values and make decisions based on those comparisons. This allows us to create more adaptable programs, assessing conditions before acting. The ability to choose from several choices based on some criteria creates complexity. This means your code management skills need to grow with your skills because you will soon be able to write bigger scripts. In addition, you will learn how to use loops.

Conditional Statements

The application is not accurate, and it lacks some functionality. Also, there are logical issues in the code, and we need to fix them. We can improve accuracy through value comparisons because if we can compare values, we can instruct the application to act differently based on those comparisons. This is what conditional statements are made for.

Conditional statements add an extra layer of sophistication. In all our examples, we have used a list of commands to achieve our ends. This will change the conditional statements. An application will be able to decide between several options the most appropriate actions as dictated by us. If a condition is met, the problem will act a certain way, and if it is not met, it will act in another way. Below is the pseudocode of conditional statements:

```
If condition is true:
    Perform these actions;
If this condition is true:
    Perform another set of actions;
If this condition is false:
    Don't do anything;
```

Look at how logical that is. This is an example of how putting our thoughts in pseudocode can make things very clear. So, make it a habit of yours. Look at how effortlessly the pseudocode above has demonstrated conditional statements. Conditional statements follow a simple structure: if x, then y.

There are several ways conditions can be checked, namely by using comparison operators listed below:

1. Less than: <

2. Less than or equal: <=

3. Greater than: >

4. Greater than or equal: >=

5. Equal: ==

6. Not equal: !=

Operators are used in a variety of ways. For example, you can write the same conditional statement using a different operator by tweaking the conditional statement's logic. Conditional statements return true or false answers when they are checked. Like below:

```
5 < 9
True
-10 >=10
False
5.5 != 5.5
False
23.56 > 78.2
False
```

Now, let's assess a conditional expression by assigning a value to a variable first:

```
myVariable = 10
myVariable == 10
True
```

As you can see, first, we used a single equals sign to assign a value. Then we used two equal signs to check if the number stored in myVariable is equal to ten. In other words, two equals signs are used to compare if values are equal, and a single one assigns values. This expression will return a Boolean value: True or False. If you use the wrong operator in a conditional statement, Python will throw an error. In some cases, using the assignment operator over the comparison operator might not lead to any errors if the assignment performed does impede a particular function's role. This is where you might think the program produces strange or wrong results.

Control Flow

Most applications need to be able to choose which section of code gets executed when something happens. To do this, you need a control flow statement. Control flow statements evaluate statements and instructions to decide how they should be executed. So far, you have learned how to compare values. But this is very useful when you can use the answer returns to direct the program. In other words, control flow statements are conditional statements because they check some condition and execute code based on the results.

Conditional statements are created by using the following keywords: if, elif, else. If you come from another language, note we don't use the "then" keyword. Now, let's look at the syntax:

```
if condition:
    #Do this
    print "This condition is true"
elif condition != True:
    #Do this instead
    print "This condition isn't true"
else:
    #Perform a default action if none of the conditions are met
    print "The condition isn't true or false"
```

The syntax above is easy to understand because we already think this way in our day to day lives. Let's examine the code.

We have an "if" conditional followed by the expression that is to be checked. The next statement, elif, means "else if." It will be checked when the first conditional returns false. The else statement is executed when all other conditions return false. In order words, it is the default; it can also be used to catch data that doesn't fit what is being assessed. If you don't set the "else" to catch something unexpected, the program will run regardless. With that said, you don't always have to use the "elif" or "else" statements. In some cases, you want a program to carry on executing or do nothing if a condition is not met. In that case, you will use an "if" statement.

Notice how the code is indented. Python requires you to do this, or you will get an error. Other programming languages rely on clear delimiters like curly braces. Python doesn't do this. Look at what happens when you don't:

```
if x:
    print (x)
    x + 1
indent = "terrible"
  File "<stdin>, line 4
indent = "terrible"
```

```
        ^
```

IndentationError: unindent does not match any outer indentation level

Conditional statements are very important. You will use them a lot in your career. Programs can use them to verify data, for example. This is called validation. You can write a program that performs a check on an item. Imagine the program would have a checklist of features an item needs to fulfill, and it ticks a box for each feature present. You can use them to check if a data set falls within a specific range. Many of what programs do would be near impossible without conditionals.

Handling Errors

Many of the scripts we have written have been simple, so they didn't require more than a test run. But as you build more complex programs, you will need to test your programs in more sophisticated ways, or you will miss pernicious bugs. Tests also help you determine if your application is competitive or really does what it seems to do. One way to test your applications is through a trace table. Trace tables are used to test algorithms or logic errors. They do this by simulating every step of your application execution, and each statement is evaluated. They look like this:

```
Step       Statement    Notes      variable1    variable2
     condition1  condition2
1
2
3
```

To see them in action, let's go back to our curtains application to see where we went wrong. We will trace variables' values and statements from beginning to end. We will replace trace table headers with variable names and program conditions. Ideally, you'd perform multiple tests with different data sets to find many other possibilities. This is because the most critical application errors occur because of abnormal values, also referred to as critical values. These are values that the application does not expect, so it has no support for them. This is why you should test vigorously to expose gaping design flaws.

In our curtain application, the crucial value is the material width, set to 150 cm. Reserving 20 cm for the hems would mean the largest width we can use for a single curtain is 130 cm. For anything larger, we would need to stitch width together and so on. We have surmised that the curtains will need to cover three-quarters of the window's width. This means one width of the material can cover a maximum of 170 cm. So, for larger windows, we would need to calculate several widths. We also need to ask ourselves other questions, like if the window is more wide than deep. It would mean turning the material, providing 15 cm of hem. But then the window's height has to be less than 125 cm.

Notice how we have to take a lot of conditions into account. The easiest way to verify them would be to set multiple potential window sizes we can check: 100 by 100, 100 by 200, and so on. You would also have to calculate results yourself to ensure the program is giving you . correct results. Let's do this:

1. Let's start with 100 x 100 as the measurement. In this case, we don't have to think about the width for obvious reasons. Taking the hem into consideration, we'd need 115 x 95 cm of material. Keep in mind that there are two possibilities here. You can measure by the width or the length. Both will produce different values. If you measure by length, you will need about 230 cm of material, and if you measure by width, you'd need 190 cm of material.

2. In the second case, the window is 100 x 200 cm. The curtains need a width of 150 cm. Because this is the width of the material, we should add 20cm for the hem and another 20 cm for the joining material. This brings our total to 190, meaning the dimensions of our curtain are 115 x 190 cm. If we measure along the length, we will need more material than when we measure along the width.

Continue calculating other cases. What we did reveals flaws in our design. When you continue further, you will realize that flipping the window's dimensions leads to material problems. Meaning if we measure along the width, it will only be worth it when the width is greater than the depth. Another condition is a depth of less than 125 cm. It's now up to the programmer to make crucial design decisions. Should you offer an option to consider material measurements along the width or keep it lengthwise? We also need to think of accuracy. It would be best to have the results rounded to the nearest half meter; this is about the final result, not the calculations.

With that information, let's create a trace table and compare data. Using print functions, it would look like this:

```
# add headers to the trace table
print()
print('\twidth\theight\twidths\ttoal\tprice')
# take the hems into account
# Before anything else, you need to convert the string to a
number variable
# If you don't, you will get an error due to using mathematical
operators on text
curtain_width = (float(window_width) * 0.75) + 20
print('\t', curtain_width)
curtain_length = float(window_height) + 15
print('\t\t', curtain_length)
# Next, you need to figure out the width of material you need
# and calculate the length of cloth needed for every curtain.
# keep all measurements in centimeters
widths = curtain_width / roll_width
print('\t\t\t', widths)
total_length = curtain_length * widths
print('\t\t\t\t', total_length)
# Don't forget you have two curtains.
```

```
# Double the material and divide by ten for result in meters
instead of centimeters
total_length = (total_length * 2) / 10
print('\t\t\t\t', total_length)
#Now we need the price in total
price = total_length * price_per_metre
print('\t\t\t\t\t', price)
```

We'll leave it here for now. Notice that we used tab to separate variable columns and organize our trace table. Now that we have this, we can test our design. Here's how it should look:

```
Enter the height of the window (cm): 100
Enter the width of the window (cm): 100
width       height        widths        total        price
95.0
115
0.678571428571
78.0357142857
15.6071428571
 78.0357142857
You need 15.6071428571 meters of cloth for 78.0357142857.
```

After our first test, we noticed a couple of issues. Our conversion to meters wasn't accurate, so our results are inaccurate. Our output has too many decimals for it to be actionable. We simply don't need that when dealing with fabric. We can solve this by using the "round" function. The round functions will take two parameters, the number to reduce decimals and the number of points we need to reduce to. In this case, two decimals points are enough. Notice that we are rounding the results, not the calculations themselves. If we try to round the calculations, this might lead to errors. With these modifications, you should get results like these:

```
You need 2.92 meters of cloth for 14.59.
```

Our output display has improved. But if we go and purchase materials using these measurements, we would end up a bit short. So, we need to know what value to expect to confirm the program is working well. Without running tests, it would be impossible to tell if our calculations are accurate and useful. While we may find our output discoursing at this point, comparing our numbers to expected values can help us figure out where we went wrong. Take some time to go through the program, run more tests, and figure out what is not working. Some fine-tuning is needed. How can we implement it?

Adding the Conditionals

To improve our program, we need to add conditional statements. We need the application to be able to measure the cloth in more than one way. For instance, if the length is smaller than the material roll's width, we can flip it and use one width of material. What do we do if the curtain should be longer and wider than the fabric rolls? Say we need a material that is equal to less than half of the width of the roll. It means we would have to buy a material roll of the same length. But if we need more than half, we would have to get two more rolls. We just described the kinds of conditions we need the program to check before it starts making calculations. Let's begin with the pseudocode. This time we will follow Python syntax:

```
if curtain width < roll width:
total_length = curtain width
else:
total_length = curtain length
if (curtain width > roll width) and (curtain length > roll
width):
if extra material < (roll width / 2):
width +=1
if extra material > (roll width / 2):
width +=2
```

We now need to calculate how many roll widths there are in certain widths and how much fabric is needed to determine an entire width. Here's how we would calculate that:

```
widths = int(curtain_width/roll_width)
additional_material = curtain_width%roll_width
```

All that was required was an integer function to remove decimals and find out how much extra material we have using the modulo operator. Now use the knowledge you have gained to improve your program. Consider repeating this process with different values.

We also use programming to make things more efficient by automating repetitive tasks. One way of achieving this is through loops. Python allows us to create loops in two ways: through the "while" statement or the "for" statement.

"While" Loops

A "while" loop starts by checking if a condition is true. A statement is executed as long as the condition is true. So it checks if it is true and executes, then it checks against and executes, and so on. Here's an example of one:

```
x = 1
while x < 10:
    print(x)
    x += 1
```

This loop checks if x is smaller than ten, then it executes code. It checks if x is still smaller and continues to execute until x is no longer smaller than ten. During the execution, the x value is incremented by one. Every execution of the code in the loop is called an iteration because it is repeated several times.

When making "while" loops, you need to be aware of two things. The variable that is checked by the loop needs to be initialized before the loop is run, and the variable needs to update/change with every iteration, or else you will have an infinite loop. Infinite loops can be dangerous, and Python won't tell you when you have created one. If you find a program is stuck in an infinite loop, you need to terminate it, but this may not work in some circumstances. Infinite loops won't damage your computer, but they can overcrowd and deplete your system's resources, causing your system to slow down or reboot. In some rare circumstances, infinite loops are helpful or desired. But it is best to avoid them as a beginner.

Conditional statements allow you to use any type of variable. Let's consider a program that calculates the mean of multiple values that the user puts in. What should be the problem that this application focuses on? The program needed to take into account the user's input because it doesn't know how many values the user will enter and if they will be positive values. To do this, we need a loop containing a sentinel value. A sentinel value signals the program to break a loop when a special value is detected. The program needs to check if the user's input value holds a value that the script would accept. For example, the loop would iterate as long as there are positive values and stop when a negative value is detected. Here's an illustration of this below:

```
offset = 0
total = 0
x = 0
while x >= 0:
    x = int (input ("Enter a positive value: "))
    total += x
    offset += 1
mean = total / offset
print (mean)
```

Another issue is that we do not know the type of values entered by the user, so we should automatically convert them into a format we can work with: integers. If a user enters a string, the program will terminate because of a value error.

Another important aspect of loops is quitting them. The "break" and "continue" methods help us break out of a loop without causing issues. For instance, you may want to quit a loop when a certain condition is met without checking other conditions. In that case, you use "break." If you want to skip a specific iteration, you can use "continue," and the loop will go to the next iteration.

In some cases, you want the program to verify a condition and not act in any specified manner. To do this, you use the "pass" keyword. The pass keyword forms a null statement, meaning the program will skip the loop and move the next code block. Here's an example below:

```
while True:
my_input = int (new_input ("$? : >> "))
if my_input > 0:
    pass
else:
    print ("This input is negative")
Now let's see an example of using break and continue:
offset = 0
total = 0
```

```
while True:
my_input = float (input ("$? : >> "))
    if my_input < 0:
        if offset == 0:
            print ("You need to enter some values!")
            continue
        break
    total += my_input
    offset += 1
    print (offset, ':', total)
```

Python allows you to nest multiple loops and conditional statements. Interestingly you can have an infinite structure of loop levels, but it is not recommended. When you nest too many loops, you can become quickly confused when errors occur. Knowing which condition a program should follow out of many options is hard. So try to keep it simple if you can. Indentation also makes things hard to read. Each loop and conditional needs to be indented, creating a large number of intricate blocks. It will look haphazard to any programmer, regardless of skill level. The general rule is to check your program from other solutions if you need to go over two looping layers. There is simply no need for such complexity. A simple solution is waiting to be found. Find it.

"For" Loops

Loops can also be created with the "for" statement. It has the same structure as the "while" loop, and in most cases, you can use both interchangeably. But for loops are best used for interaction over a sequence like lists, dictionaries, and strings. In the first iteration, the first element in the sequence is retrieved, then the second, and so forth.

To understand "for" loops, you need to understand a few basics about sequences. We will talk more about sequences in the next chapter, but we have already worked with one: strings: Strings are just a sequence of characters. There are also lists, which are sequences of elements that are manipulated. There are also tuples, which are similar to lists but cannot be edited. Below is an example of a "for" loop:

```
buildings = ["store", "house", "hospital", "school"]
for x in buildings:
    print (x)
```

Each element in the list will be printed. You can also loop through a string, like this:

```
for x in "store":
    print (x)
```

Every character in "store" will be printed individually.

We can break "for" loops just as we would with "while" loops. Below we stop the loop when "hospital" is found in the list.

```
buildings = ["store", "house", "hospital", "school"]
for x in buildings:
    print (x)
    if x == "hospital":
        break
```

As you can see, the break occurs after "hospital" is printed. Below is another case:

```
buildings = ["store", "house", "hospital", "school"]
for x in buildings:
    if x == "hospital":
        break
    print (x)
```

In this example, the loop breaks before "hospital" is printed. Next is the "continue" keyword that will skip a specified iteration, in this case "hospital":

```
buildings = ["store", "house", "hospital", "school"]
for x in buildings:
    if x == "hospital":
        continue
    print (x)
As you can see, each element is printed except "hospital".
```

Summary

In this chapter, we learned how to make programs more intelligent. Many basic tasks require us to use logical operators, comparison operators, and assignment operators. We have also learned how to use loops and conditional statements to introduce decision making.

Improving designing with conditionals and loops is a common feature in programming. Use these tools to improve your program. We also looked at trace tables and how they help with logic error detections. Lastly, programming itself is where you design, program, test, and repeat until you solve a problem.

In the next chapter, we will look at Python data structures and how to manipulate them.

CHAPTER 5:

Python Data Structures

Data structures are fundamental to any programming language. We are going to look at working with lists, tuples, dictionaries, and strings. We are going to create a more complex program to illustrate their use. We will build a game since games use data structures for character statistics and inventory. We will also need to calculate combat results and turn them into textual data. We will build on the knowledge from previous chapters, so don't fret. You will also get good practice with loops and conditionals.

Our design and development discussion will continue, especially now when working with a more complex program. A game requires many mathematical operations and textual data, and Python is great for that. Until now, we have only focused on using code to produce basic outputs. In the real world, programs are more complex than that. They involve complex structures that demand a huge number of statements. When you know Python's data structures well, you will be able to simplify the process. Data structures like tuples, lists, dictionaries, and strings will help in that regard.

Sequences

As we said, strings, lists, and tuples are examples of sequences. There are many ways of accessing data inside sequences. First, we should analyze data structures. Data structures that can be modified are called mutable. They have mutability. Strings and tuples cannot be modified, so they are immutable. But we can use tuples and strings to form new ones. Lists are mutable because we can add and delete elements they host.

So, how do we access elements in a sequence? We can use the index of an item. Indexes represent the position of an element. Indexes are written as an integer inside square brackets. Below is an example:

```
building = "hospital"
building[0]
"h"
```

Below is an example with a list. Each position has an index starting from 0:

```
buildings = ["store", "house", "hospital", "school"]
buildings [2]
"hospital"
```

Since the indexes start at zero, "hospital" is in the second position. Indexes starting from zero is a common feature in programming. This is why 2 accesses the third element in the list. You can also use negative integers to access items:

```
buildings[-1]
"school"
```

Negative indexes start counting from the end of the list or string.

How do you access multiple elements at the same time? You use slicing to do it. You can slice a part of the sequence by entering two indexes. The first index indicates where the slice should begin; the second chooses where the slice should end. So a slice like this [1:4] means the slice will start at the second position and end at the fifth position in the list. You can also access them in reverse. You can also ignore entering the first element. Python will assume it should start the element in the first position. The same thing will happen if you leave the second value empty.

```
[:3]
[3:]
```

The slice method created a new sequence, meaning the original data will not get changed. You will be able to manipulate and work with the elements in the original list. So if you edit an element in the parent sequence and the sliced sequence, they will change. Editing is different from slicing because it mutates sequences.

Sequence Check

Sometimes you will need to check if an item is part of a sequence. You can do this with the "in" keyword. This keyword returns a Boolean value. True means the item is present, and False means the item is not in the sequence. Below is the example of the code; we are using it against the buildings list we created earlier:

```
"pear" in buildings
False
```

You can also use the "not" keyword to ask if the item is not in the list. In this instance, True would mean the item is not present, and False would mean it is.

```
"pear" not in buildings
True
```

You can also use an addition operator to combine sequences:

```
"sun" + "flower"
"sunflower"
```

You can also use the join() method to do the same thing. In programming, there are many ways of doing the same thing. Data types dictate what type of functions, methods, and operators can be used. But most will use the plus sign, minus sign, "in", "or" keywords, and so on.

We haven't discussed method syntax yet. Methods are placed next to the variable they perform on, connected by a dot/period. Methods can also contain arguments inside parentheses. Here's an example: separator.join(seq), This is the join method. Methods are bound to a specific object/data type. You will understand this more as we discuss objects and methods in the next chapter. For now, keep in mind that an object is a data type that has many instances.

Regarding strings, the sequence that is being added to the string is received as an argument passed through the parentheses. We will get a single string as a result. Here's how it would look:

```
", ".join (buildings)
"store, house, hospital, school"
```

To improve readability, you can change it by adding "sep=","" and then call the join method.

We can also divide a string into a list. This is called splitting. It can be done with the split method. Here's an example below:

```
string.split(separator, max).
```

The second argument specifies how many times the string should be split.

```
buildings = "store, house, hospital, school, church "
buildings = buildings.split(", ")
buildings [ 'store', 'house', 'hospital', 'school', 'church']
```

The split above splits the string at every comma in the string. You can split a string at every space or whatever character you prefer. We can then manipulate the list in whatever way we want. We can also use the list method to convert a string into a list. Below, we convert a string into a list of characters:

```
list ('house')
['h', 'o', 'u', 's', 'e']
```

Below we convert a list into a tuple:

```
tuple (buildings)
( 'store', 'house', 'hospital', 'school', 'church')
```

Below we convert a list into a string:

```
str (buildings)
"[ 'store', 'house', 'hospital', 'school', 'church']"
```

We can also use "len" to get the length of an element. It will return how many elements are in a sequence. This is useful when faced with a long list containing thousands of elements. Here's how it looks:

```
len (buildings)
5
```

Max and min will return the highest and lowest element in order. Here's how it looks:

```
max (buildings)
'store'
min (buildings)
church
```

The max method did not return the highest index item; it returned the highest alphabetically. If this list contained numbers, it would choose the highest in ascending order. The elements have a default hierarchy even though they occupy different points as far as indexes are concerned. Because of this, you can use a comparison operator to compare several sequences. Imagine you have two sentences. The second is called "jobs," and it has five elements. If you compare both, Python will decide one is bigger than the other. Here's the code below:

```
jobs > buildings
False
buildings == jobs
False
```

If you try this with an empty sequence, you will always get a False result.

Tuples

Earlier, we said tuples are immutable data structures. They are like lists, but they cannot be modified. So, they are data packs that contain locked information.

Tuples contain a list of values separated by commas, contained in parentheses instead of square brackets. Parentheses aren't always necessary, but you should use them to avoid errors and confusion. Tuples can also contain values that are not of the same data type. Tuples can also contain other tuples, or nothing at all. Here's an example of an empty tuple:

```
emptyTuple = ()
```

The tuple below contains an element.:

```
lonelyTuple = ('element')
```

Tuples have sequences like lists. Their purpose is to pass specific values to something else without changing its state.

Lists

Lists contain elements that are separated by commas inside square brackets. Lists are mutable and can contain a variety of data types, including other lists. Mutability allows them to be concatenated, indexed, sliced, assigned new values, and so forth. Essentially, you can do whatever you want with lists. Below is an example of a list:

```
character_inventory = ['sword', ['more', 'lists'], 'bag of gold', '2
healing potions']
You can add a new element by indexing, just like below:
character_inventory[1] = 'leather armor'
character_inventory ['sword', 'leather armor', 'bag of gold', '2
healing potions']
You can also replace parts of a list with another list. Here's
how:
character_inventory[::2] = ['spell scroll', 'healing herb', 'pet
rock']
character_inventory ['spell scroll', 'leather armor', 'healing
herb', 'bag of gold', 'pet rock']
```

We didn't clarify where the new slice should start or end. We only said it should have a step size equal to two, meaning every second item should be affected.

These are some other methods that allow us to add new elements to the list: "append" and "extend." "Append" adds new elements, and "extend" adds elements from another list. Here are examples of both:

```
character_inventory.append ('raw meat')
character_inventory ['spell scroll', 'leather armor', 'healing
herb',
'bag of gold', 'pet rock', 'raw meat']
character_inventory.extend (['mace', 'flask'])
character_inventory ['spell scroll', 'leather armor', 'healing
herb',
'bag of gold', 'pet rock', 'raw meat', 'mace', 'flask']
```

The "del" keyword lets us delete elements. You should know that "del" does not remove the data itself from the list. It moves the reference to a certain item if used in another data structure. Nothing changes internally.

```
del character_inventory [4:]
character_inventory
```

```
['spell scroll', 'leather armor', 'healing herb', 'bag of gold']
```

A section of the list, starting from the fourth element, was removed. Let's add an element to the list the following way:

```
character_inventory.insert(2,'staff')
character_inventory
['spell scroll', 'leather armor', 'staff', 'healing herb', 'bag of
gold']
```

We have added an element at index 2 after the second element. Let's now delete a specific element from the list:

```
character_inventory.remove ('leather armor')
character_inventory
['spell scroll', 'staff', 'healing herb', 'bag of gold']
```

In some cases, you want to delete an item and return its value while you do. You can do it by using two methods or with one command. The latter is the simpler method so we should choose it. The "pop" method does this for us. It takes an index of the element as the argument and removes it after returning it. If you do not enter an index, the pop method will remove the last in the list. Look at the example below:

```
character_inventory.pop(-2)
'healing herb'
character_inventory
['spell scroll', 'staff', 'healing herb', 'bag of gold']
```

The negative index allows us to remove the second to last element after returning its value.

Now, let's sort lists. Lists can be sorted in two ways: "sort" and "sorted" methods. The sort method will mutate the list, meaning the action is performed on the actual list. The "sorted" method will copy the original list, sort the copy, and return it, meaning the original list does not change. These methods look the same even in the results they output. Still, it is important to understand this difference because it can affect how your application will react. Below are examples:

```
sorted(character_inventory)
['bag of gold', 'healing herb', 'staff', 'spell scroll']
character_inventory.sort()
To reverse the order of the list, we use the "reverse" method:
reversed (character_inventory)
<listreverseiterator object at 0x81abf0c>
character_inventory.reverse()
character_inventory
['spell scroll', 'staff', 'healing herb', 'bag of gold']
```

Remember that some methods and functions will not return another sequence but will return an object. In our example, we have an iterator object commonly used in "for" loops as if it is a sequence. When we used the "reversed" function, we got a reverse iterator object. Look below:

```
for element in reversed(character_inventory):
print item
spell scroll
staff
healing herb
bag of gold
```

Matrix

A matrix is a multidimensional list. Multidimensional lists are essentially nested lists, or lists inside a list. This allows us to hold tabular data. Below is an example of a nested list:

```
my_matrix = [[11, 12, 13], [21, 22, 23], [31, 32, 33]]
```

This is a three by three matrix. If you remember elementary math, this is not new to you.

You should use the "for" loop to iterate through a list, especially if you aren't sure how many elements are in the list. But how do you iterate through a matrix like the one above? You would need to use a "for" loop inside a "for" loop. A nested loop to access the nested list. The "enumerate" function will give you index values. Let's look at a list example and a matrix one for comparison:

```
for x, value in enumerate (character_inventory):
print x, value
0 spell scroll
1 staff
2 healing herb
3 bag of gold
Now let's see the matrix version:
for row in matrix:
for x, value in enumerate(row):
print i, value,
print
0 11 1 21 2 31
0 21 1 22 2 32
0 31 1 32 2 33
```

Dictionaries

Dictionaries work the same way as yellow pages. As long as you have a name, you will be able to gather all the other contact information about the person. When it comes to dictionaries, names are keys, and the information is called values. Keys are immutable, and they can only be strings, tuples, or numbers. Values can be any kind of supported data. Although keys are not mutable, dictionaries themselves are mutable, meaning you can edit them. Dictionaries are also known as mappings because keys are mapped to specific objects.

If you come from another programming language, you will know that data types like dictionaries are known as hashes or associative arrays. There are differences because values that determine keys are hash values. What is meant by this? Hashed keys can be stored in larger keys because they are small values defined from the key. It might be confusing, but what you should understand is that Python arranges dictionary data by hash keys instead of alphabetical order. So, if you change a value, the hash resulting from the change will be modified, and the program won't find the value. This is why keys cannot be changed.

Now, let's take a look at some code. Remember that dictionaries are defined by key-value pairs, separated by colons, and enclosed in curly braces. Don't confuse brackets, parentheses, and curly braces; they have different effects. With that said, here's an example:

```
character_profile = {'Name':"",'Description':"", 'Race':"",
'Sex':"",'Strength':0,'Intellect':0,'Dexterity':0,'Charisma':0}
character_profile['Name'] = "Player"
print character_profile['Name'], "has",
character_profile['Intellect'], "Intellect"
Player has 0 Intellect
```

When you pass a reference to one of the elements, you will need to use square brackets. Just remember that dictionaries don't use indexes that tell us where an element position is. Dictionaries use key and value pairs instead; we use a value's key to find it. The syntax is like this: "[dictionary [key] = value]. The name of the key has to be inside quotation marks or Python will think it is a variable. The "for" loop can be used to iterate a dictionary. This further demonstrates the usefulness of loops. Below is an example:

for key in character_profile:

```
print(key)
```

Intellect Name Sex Race Charisma Strength Dexterity Description

When you want to access a value, you use the following syntax: "character_profile [key]". If you need to find out if a certain key exists, you will have to look for it in the profile. The check will return a Boolean value or an error. You would use the following method to find out if a key exists:

```
get (key, default)
```

As you can see, the method accepts arguments. The first argument is the key we are looking for, and the second is the default value if the key doesn't exist. Let's look at some code:

```
character_profile.get('Name')
'Player'
character_profile.get('Sex', 'unknown')
''
character_profile.get('Health', 'not found')
'not found'
```

As you can see, we have the key, but there is an empty value instead of a string. Below we delete an element from the dictionary:

```
character_profile {'Name': 'Player', 'Sex': '', 'Race': '',
'Charisma': 0, 'Strength': 0, 'Dexterity': 0, 'Description': ''}
del character_profile['Sex']
character_profile
{'Name': 'Player', 'Race': '', 'Charisma': 0, 'Strength': 0,
'Dexterity': 0, 'Description': ''}
```

As you can see, we have to use the del method to delete an element from the dictionary. Just like with sequences, you can use the "pop" method to delete a value. You use the "sorted" method to sort a dictionary.

Dictionaries are important data structures. You can almost find them in any program relying on attributes that have values. You can even make a dictionary that stores states of an object, meaning you won't make duplicates. Therefore, you can use them to store input data and results from the operations we perform. For example, you might want to find out how many times a letter appears in a sentence, then iterate through individual letters, assigning each to a key.

Creating a Basic Game

We will now create a basic game that will apply all we have learned about sequences. This will build on the character generator we made earlier. Before we get to it, let's start with design.

We'll separate the code into three blocks. You'll need to generate character stats, purchase gear, and do battle. Let's explore these further:

1. We need to store character stats. This requires us to have a container. A dictionary is a good choice for this. A player will be able to choose their name, description, sex, and race. Character stats — strength, dexterity, charismas, and gold — will be random. There will be a set of other stats that track health, mana, and armor. To generate these numbers, we need to use a random module. We haven't explored modules yet. They can be explained as a compilation of functions we call to perform specific tasks. Python modules are imported into the project where they can be used like regular methods and functions. Think of them as extensions.

2. In the second section, we will define a "trader" where players will spend gold for items. We will also use a dictionary for this. Trader items will have keys, and prices will be the values paired with them.

3. Lastly, we will have a combat system that allows characters to select weapons and attack each other. We also want the amount dealt to be displayed in the text, meaning we will need multiple tuples. We will need to figure out how we deal with weapon damage calculations; we will cheat a little here. Then we will give our character two more items: "attack damage" and "attack speed." We will also have tuples with price, attack damage, and attack speed. These will not change since they are stored in

tuples. We need to add them at the beginning of the program to get them over with. We also need the battle to take until one character dies, which means we will loop the phase until we get one result or another.

Now that we have a basic idea of what our program needs to look like, we can begin our second phase by writing pseudocode:

```
# declare the constant variables that don't change their values
# define the trader = {}
#1 while characters < 2
#1.1 declare character profile dictionary
#1.2 Ask the user to insert the following information about
their character
# (Name', 'Description', 'Sex', 'Race')
#1.3 Confirm data
#1.4 Implement random stats generation
#('Strength', 'Intellect', 'Dexterity', 'Charisma')
#1.5 Implement secondary character stats
#('health', 'mana', 'armor', 'gold')
## Allow the user to modify certain stats
#1.6 Confirm the character stats
#1.7 Display character stats document
#1.8 Ask the player to buy some gear from the trader
#1.9 loop while purchase not equal to 'no.'
#1.9.1 Display trader's item list with prices.
#1.9.2 Ask the user to buy items.
#1.9.3 If the player has enough gold and
#the trader has the item available, buy the item.
#1.10 Introduce another player
## Combat section
# Prepare the lists with descriptive text.
## hits = (), misses = (), damage_taken = (), health_update = ()
#2 Players enter battle.
## Player decides which weapon to use.
## As long as the weapon is in his inventory.
## If the selected weapon doesn't exist, the player will use his
fists.
#3 Loop while opponent [health] > 0 and target[health] > 0:
#3.1 for player in battle:
#3.1.1 Calculate the attack speed
#3.1.2 Calculate the attack damage
#3.1.3 Print damage taken
#3.1.4 if opponent [health] > 0 and target [health] > 0: break
#3.2 Print player progress
 #4 Print winner
```

This program is much more complex than anything we have done so far. Before continuing, pay attention to the pseudocode's structure. The more complicated a design is, the more time you have to spend in preparation. Also, don't look at an application as a monolith. Break it up into smaller, more manageable tasks. Then go through it one by one.

We can easily translate the pseudocode above into Python. We start with constant variables then import the random statement. Then we set "trader" dictionary items. Each element will contain three tuples for price, attack damage, and speed. Then we will set other purchasable elements like armor and weapons, followed by four tuples. They'll hold text describing weapon hits, misses, damage reports, and health updates. Since this is a game, you can get creative with the descriptive text. It needs to fit with the game and goals of your characters.

Then we'll have a list that will hold player profiles. The list will be called "players." These profiles will be temporarily hosted inside the characer_profile dictionary. The user will be presented with four fields where they will enter information about their character. Afterward, we use the random module "random.randint (start, end)" to generate player stats. The module is a random number generator. The secondary stats are generated from these numbers, verified to ensure they fall between 1 and 100 to simplify things. If the number generated does not fall within a range, the dice is thrown again until a valid number is found. After the code block, the character sheet is printed.

Then we have the item purchasing section, which can be attached to the character generator. This simplifies the code and tightens the designs. We can also use the "for" loop to loop through purchasable items. We'll access the price of the items in the tuple. The player will be able to finalize the purchase. When they do, the item will be added to their inventory. Gold will be subtracted for the item. The player will be asked to select a weapon from their inventory. If they don't have one, the default will be their fists. Behind the scenes, the player accesses the tuple from the trader dictionary and converts it to a weapon value. It's the same with armor values. All this data allows us to build a profile.

Fighting occurs in a while loop that ends when one of the characters loses their health. Inside is another loop that swaps turns between the fighters since this is a turn-based combat mechanism. The loop accesses a player's index and turns it into a Boolean. After a turn, the "not" operator reverses the value, meaning the attacker/target index is swapped between characters.

Another aspect is the attack speed calculation. A player has to roll a positive number to hit the target; negative numbers are misses. We've set the range between zero and seven. This is important. The value will be confirmed in the misses and hits tuple. A result will be printed depending on whether an attack is landed or not. Then we use that value for damage calculation. Remember, these values are set within a slightly random range, within limits, to make the game more fun and unpredictable.

The last section will describe how much health is taken from the attack. Then their health is updated to reflect that loss. If it is not a negative value or zero, the game continues. The loop breaks when zero or a negative number is reached. Then we have a winner, and the program stops.

Coding Exercise

You know enough to attempt coding this. You have detailed pseudocode and a full explanation of all its parts, so give it a shot. There is nothing else you have to learn to do this. Yes, seriously. Just look at what was learned in this chapter, and it should be simple enough to do.

Sure it's intimidating, but you need to practice without scaffolding now and then. Don't just copy and test. Write the code yourself and see what happens. It's how you learn. Even in failure, you will learn a lot. If you get stuck, go online and seek help from other developers. Chances are someone has faced your problem and solved it, and people are willing to help.

Summary

In this chapter, we have learned to work with Python data structures like dictionaries, tuples, and lists. We saw how we could apply them in useful scenarios. It might have been overwhelming in some parts, but we put our heads up and slogged the marsh.

We know the difference between mutable and immutable sequences. We can access elements with indexes and slicing, edit lists, and iterate through sequences using loops. They looked weird at first, but now we understand how essential they are to building more powerful, logical programs.

But most important of all, we built a really impressive program. And we did it on our own. Well, almost. We have started to develop our research skills, which are indispensable in careers like this one. It's our first taste of what it's like to work in the real world, with all its highs and lows.

CHAPTER 6:

Functions

We've worked with variables, done arithmetic, and worked with comparison and decision making. We can write basic scripts. But have you noticed one downside to all the code we have been doing? If we change a part of the code, we will have to change all of the code. Everything needs to be precise. This is because our lines of code are like one big block of code, or a list of instructions that needs to be performed line by line. And if the program needs to perform a task, it has to start all over again. That is bad design. What happens if you want to update just one part of the code? You need to go through all of it. You can see how this cannot be how modern applications work. It's not very efficient. This is where functions come in. Essentially, functions divide your code into chunks that perform specific tasks. In this chapter, we are going to learn about how they work so we can improve our programs.

Creating Functions

We've already worked with in-built Python functions or methods. But they aren't enough. So, we have to build our own functions. Don't worry; all functions are built the same way, even the in-built ones.

Functions come with a lot of advantages:

- Like we have said, you can divide your code, so updating and maintaining your code becomes easier in the long run. You won't have to go through the rest of your project whenever you make a change.

- Functions eliminate code redundancy. You won't have to write or use the same code a lot of times. The rule is if you have to write a piece of code more than twice, turn it into a function. This will make your job simpler, and your code will be a lot more readable. All you will need to do, whenever you need the same code or task

49

performed, is to call the function.

- In a team, they allow you to split a program into manageable sections that can be developed independently. This means the work will be done much faster. In the end, all the code is connected.

Let's look at a project that is written with functions. Like we said, projects are the best way to learn. We will be building a tic tac toe game, where users will play against a computer. We'll start with game instructions. These will be written as a separate program. Let's look at the code below:

```
# game guide
# illustrating user-defined functions
def gameGuide ():
    '''Display instructions. '''
    print (
    '''Welcome to the most epic game you will ever play!
    This will be a battle of wits between you, the fleshy
creature.
    Against I, the all-knowing computer!
    You will start by entering a number from 0 to 8,
```

which will correspond to the following positions on the game board:

```
0 | 1 | 2
3 | 4 | 5
6 | 7 | 8
Prepare for battle! \n ''')
# main
print("This is the game guide for Tic Tac Toe: ")
gameGuide()
print("Review them once more:")
gameGuide () print("Surely you understand how it works.")
input("\n\n Press the enter key to quit.")
Now let's analyze the code in the next section.
```

Function Definition

Functions should be defined before they can be used. They are defined using the "def" keyword. In our last example, it looked like this:

```
def gameGuide ():
```

So, what do we mean by define? It's a way of telling the computer that the next block of code belongs to the function which we have given a name. We will be able to access the code by calling the function. The information inside functions tells it what it should do. Python will know of all functions inside the program, so you can call it whenever you need it. Just remember that functions will not work unless they are called.

Functions are called by their name and parentheses, like this:

```
gameGuide()
```

In our example, we did this a couple of times. And whenever we did this, the program printed the game guide.

The syntax is easy to follow. All you really need is the def keyword, followed by your choice of name, parentheses, and a colon. The parentheses can hold parameters; we haven't used those yet, but we will. Then below, you write statements you want to be executed by the function.

Function Documentation

You can document functions with a documentation string, also known as the docstring. In our game guide, it looks like this:

```
"""Display instructions."""
```

See, we used triple quotes as we do with comments when we do a block of text. Docstrings have to be written in the first line after the definition. In our example, we wrote a sentence describing the purpose of the function. Documentation isn't necessary. But it is useful, especially when you are making a larger number of functions. You might need a reminder of what they do, especially if you work in a team. Docstrings can also be accessed in IDLE, where you can review their function, the same when you do with built-in functions.

Using Parameters

You've noticed with default Python functions that we can set values and have them return values. For instance, using the "len" function to get the length value. The same thing can be done with defined functions.

Let's look at a small program that uses three defined functions. It'll show different ways of obtaining and returning values. We will set one function to receive a value and another to return a function. Then the third function will do both. Below is the code:

```
# Parameters and Values
# Exploring the use of parameters
def show (message):
print (message)
def return_me_ten():
ten = 10
return ten
def ask_yes_or_no (question):
"""Ask a yes or no question."""
response = None
while response not in ("y", "n"):
response = input(question).lower()
return response
# main
show("You have a message.\n")
number = return_me_ten()
print("This is what I received from return_me_ten():", number)
```

```
answer = ask_yes_or_no ("\nPlease enter 'y' or 'n': ")
print("Thank you:", answer)
input("\n\nPress the enter key to quit.")
```

In the sample above, we've defined the "show" function to print the value it receives through the parameters. Parameters are essentially variables within functions. Parameters obtain values sent through the call of a function. So in our first function, the "message" parameter is assigned the string "You have a message.\n." The message parameters receive the strings, and the function uses it as a variable. If the parameter had no value assigned, we would get an error. In the example above, the "show" function has one parameter, but functions can have more than one or none at all. Multiple parameters are separated by commas inside the parentheses.

Our second function is the "retun_me_ten" and uses the "return" statement to return a value. "Return ten" will send the value to the part of the application that called it. Functions terminate when they reach the "return" statement. Functions can also return multiple values separated by commas.

The third function, "ask_yes_or_no," will receive a question and answer with either yes(y) or no(n). The question will be passed through the parameter. Then it receives a value of an argument and sends it to the function. The example we have has the string: "\nPlease enter 'y' or 'n'." Then we use the argument to ask the user to respond:

```
response = None
while response not in ("y", "n"):
    response = input(question).lower()
```

We need to have a loop that repeatedly executes this section until an answer is given. Once we have a response, the arguments will be sent back to the section that called it. After the answer is returned, the function is terminated, and the program prints the answers.

Reusing Functions

Let's take a break from all the theory and coding and talk about the reusability of user-defined functions.

An upside to creating functions is that you can save them and use them in other scripts, even in other projects. In our example, we had the user give a positive or negative answer. A task like this is so common that you might want to use it in many other programs you will build.

You can do this by copying and pasting, but this is not very efficient. Remember when we talked about Python modules that you can import to extend the functionality? You can make your own modules and use them in other programs. They work the same way as standard modules. We will talk about it more later. For now, we will stick to copying and pasting.

When you are just learning, you can do whatever you like, and optimization isn't a priority. When programming in the real world, you'll need to be as efficient as possible. Writing code takes time, and you don't want to waste time. This is why you shouldn't try to reinvent the wheel. Software companies focus a lot on reusable code and making new techniques that will implement old things in new things. Here's why code reusability is important:

- It will improve the pace at which you and your team finish projects. You will also be able to build other building blocks that will speed up future development.

- It creates consistency. We may be adaptable, but a lot of time is used trying to come up with new ways of doing things. Even something like working with a new interface can slow us down and confuse us.

Global Variables

The functions we've used are closed off from each other and independent. That is why we love them. They allow us to move them about and connect them with whatever we feel like. To access data inside them, we need to use parameters. To do that, they should return a value. That's how it's mostly done. But there's another way.

We can share between sections of an application using global variables. To understand what global variables are, we need to understand scopes.

Scopes

As we've seen. It is desirable to divide programs into sections that can be accessed independently from one another. This is what we mean by scopes. With every function we create, we make a scope. That is why a function cannot directly access another function's variables. Here's a simple representation of this:

```
def function_1 ():
        variable_1
#End of the first function's scope
def function_2 ():
        variable2
#End of second function's scope
```

#This represents the global scope for the entire application

```
variable()
```

In the example above, we have three scopes. By default, programs have a global scope. In our example, we have two scopes defined by two functions. But what does all this mean?

When you aren't doing anything inside, the two functions are inside the global scope. The variables defined in this space are called global variables. Any other variables defined within a function block belong to the function and area called local variables. In our example, "variable 1" is inside the first function, making it a local variable. So, we cannot gain access to it from another scope, like the second function of the global scope. We can't even modify it.

A scope is like a car with tinted glass. If you are inside the car, you can see everything inside and outside. But if you are outside, you can't see anything inside the car. That's how functions work. These variables are inside their functions(cars), and they are invisible from the global scope(outside the car). In cases where we have many variables with the same name that belong to different functions, they will contain different data and be invisible to each other, causing no naming conflicts. So, if we had "variable2" inside the first functions and "variable2" in the second, they would be different from each other, holding different data.

Handling Global Variables

We'll write a short program to illustrate how functions can read and edit global variables, then we will analyze the code. Here's the code below:

```
#Playing with global variables
def read_global ():
    print ("From within read_global(), value is:", value)
def shadow_global ():
    value = -10
    print ("From within shadow_global(), value is:", value)
def change_global ():
    global value
    value = -10
    print ("From within change_global(), value is:", value)
#main
#From here on we are inside the global scope
#Value becomes a global variable
value = 10
print ("Within the global scope, value is: ", value, "\n")
read_global ()
print ("Within the global scope, value is set to: ", value,
"\n")
shadow_global ()
print ("Within the global scope, value is set to: ", value,
"\n")
change_global ()
print ("Within the global scope, value is now: ", value, "\n")
input("\n\nPress the enter key to quit.")
```

Reading Global Variables

We've looked at local and global variables and talked about scope. It's time to confuse you, but only a little. You can read global variables no matter what scope you are in. You can read a variable inside a function while you are in the global scope, and vice versa. It's just like we said about tinted car windows. When you are inside a car you can see everything inside, but you can also see what is out there. So a function can read global variables.

The program we wrote earlier illustrates readability. We have defined a function called "read_global," which prints values of the global variables. It works without any errors, but there's a catch. You can read these variables, but you cannot make any changes to them directly. So if you were to try, like we see below, you would get an error:

```
value += 1
```

Shadowing Global Variables

Looking at the example above, you might have wondered what the "shadow" stood for. Shadowing is giving a local variable a similar name to a global variable. But you cannot edit the global variable still. Any change you make happens to the local variable. The local variable is the shadow of the global variable, thus "shadowing." Here's how we assigned a value to the shadow_global function:

```
value = -10
```

The global value hasn't changed. But an identical local version was created inside the functions, and now that version has the value of -10. You can see this in action because we have told the program to print the global version.

But remember, shadowing like this is not always a good idea. Why? They are confusing. You probably experienced this as you were trying to figure out which is which when you look at the program.

Changing Global Variables

You can use the global "global" keyword to access global keywords. In our example, we used it to change the value to -10. When executing a value, the new value will be printed.

So when should we use global variables? The truth is that you can use them whenever you want. But is it wise? Just because you can do something doesn't mean you should. You need to weigh the pros and cons and ask yourself if it is appropriate for your project. Global variables are often problematic because they can be confusing. Use them when you absolutely have to, when you can't find a better alternative to what you are trying to achieve.

Alternatively, you can turn global variables into constants, which aren't difficult to track. Say in a tax calculator you'll have a number of functions, but all of them will use .45 as a value. You should place the value inside a global constant instead, meaning we no longer need to call the value inside every function. It might not seem like much, but it makes a big difference when working on a complex project. Having clear variables instead of numbers, that might as well be arbitrary, is much more meaningful and easier to work with.

Writing Tic Tac Toe

Earlier, we said we were going to build a Tic Tac Toe game. We will do that now that you know what functions are. Before we start coding, let's work on a thorough plan for our game. Yes, maybe it's boring, but we have to do it.

We will use functions in this game, and we will combine them with the skills we've already learned. The pseudocode won't be as detailed because we have functions that have a way of making things simpler. Here's the pseudocode below:

```
# Print the game guide
# Determine who starts
# Build the game board and display it
# While there's no winner or tie
# If it's the player's turn,
# get his move
# Update the board and display it
# Otherwise
    # Get the AI's move
    # Update the board and display it
# Swap turns
# Declare the winner
```

We know what the game is about, and we know we have to think of concrete definitions. How will the game board be presented, and how will pieces move? The first thing we need is the board. Pieces can be displayed by characters, named x and o. The board can be a list since lists are mutable. So we'll need a list that has 9 elements because a Tic Tac Toe board has nine spaces. Each element will be a representation of the board. Like this:

```
0 | 1 | 2
3 | 4 | 5
6 | 7 | 8
```

Remember that indexes start from zero. This is why our elements do, too. So each square has a number assigned to it. Moves players make are represented by a number. When it comes to Players, humans will use "X," and the computer will use "O." Then we need a variable that will tell us whose turn it is.

Adding Functions

So we got the basics of the design down. We now need to create a plan for the list of functions we will need before coding. This will allow us to brainstorm and think of the parameters they will need. Here's that list:

- game_guide (): Display the rules of the game and the instructions.

- ask_yes_or_no (question): Ask the player a question that can be answered with a yes or a no.

- ask_number (question, low, high): Ask the player for a number within a range. As you can see, we have a question parameter which the user receives, and a number will be returned. This number will be within a range from low to high.

- game_piece (): This function will represent the two pieces on the board. One belongs to the human player and the other to the AI.

- empty_board(): Create a new board.

- display_board (board): Display the board on the screen.

- allowed_moves (board): This will return a list of moves that are allowed once the board is returned.

- winner (board): Declaring the winner.

- player_move (board, player): Retrieves the move from the human player. The board and the player's piece are received, and the move is returned.

- computer_move (board, computer, player): Calculates the AI's move, the board, and the two pieces. Returns the AI's move.

- next_turn (turn): Swap turns.

- anounce_winner (winner, computer, player): Declares the winner, as well as a tie.

Setup and Exercise

We'll need to first define the global constants. Because their values don't change, you can declare them right at the beginning. This will make it easy for you when you write your functions because they are all in one place. Here's some code to get you started:

global constants

```
X = "X"
O = "O"
EMPTY = " "
TIE = "TIE"
NUM_POSITIONS = 9
```

X and O represent pieces that the player and the computer will use. The "EMPTY" constant points to empty spaces on the board. Its value is an empty space, because they need to look empty when the game starts. The "TIE" constant represents a situation where a win for either human or computer is impossible. The "NUM_POSITIONS" represent squares on the board.

This is all you need to build a tic tac toe game. Using everything you learned, you will be able to tackle this project. You have a detailed plan to carry through it, you know what functions are needed and how they should work, and we have set up global constants for you. Good luck!

Summary

In this chapter, we've learned about functions and how to write them. We also learned about scopes and the differences between global variables and local variables. We saw the importance of documenting functions and using as few global constants as possible. We topped it off by building a game of tic tac toe, showcasing a component development approach.

CHAPTER 7:

Introduction to Object-Oriented Programming

Python is considered an object-oriented programming language. What does that mean?

OOP, for short, is a new programming paradigm that has become the standard in software and game development. Most of the programs we use today use OOP. OOP is defined as the object. In this chapter, we will learn about the concepts that make up OOP. We'll explore:

- Defining objects and creating classes.

- Writing methods and declaring an object's attributes.

- Polymorphism.

- Creating modules.

Classes

Classes are the foundation of OOP. Essentially, a class is a template for building your own data type. To have a simpler time digesting this, don't think of data types like numbers or text. Think of something like a car, which can be a data type with attributes like brand model, color, and so on.

Classes allow you to make objects that you can use in projects. They are one of the most fundamental concepts in programming. It is often the last step in most programming courses. The content in the data represent attributes, and statements/commands are methods.

It might be overwhelming to wrap your head around. But OOP makes long, difficult programs easier because it decreases the work you have to do. It allows you to reuse almost all of your code. Objects can inherit attributes and methods from other classes, making it easier to modify and create new objects. So we can have a generic object and build an entire family emanating from it. In the end, we would have something like a family tree.

Say you have Flora, Fauna, and Minerals as foundational classes. They will have attributes that will be passed to any object belonging to them. Classes allow you to create a subclass. For instance, the Fauna parent class has Bird and Fish as subclasses. Bird and Fish will inherit some attributes from the Fauna class, which makes it distinct from other classes.

On top of that, Bird and Fish will also have their own attributes, which make them different. You can create another subclass, say a Chicken or Raven subclass, that inherits attributes from the Bird Class. Suppose we have to create an instance of the Raven class that we give the name Charlie. Charlie will inherit all the attributes that Raven has, like the "caw()" method. So when we write "charlie.caw()," we would get the string "Caw! Caw!" as the output.

Objects, classes, and methods resemble the ways we think about the world. That is why developers favor object orientated programming. It allows them to think straightforwardly.

Python Namespaces

We need to learn how to define classes before we take a closer look at them. This is why we have to look at namespaces first, so we understand object-oriented programming a little deeper.

Namespaces map names to an object. By default, namespaces are Python dictionaries. An example of a namespace is a collection of default names containing functions like "abs." The namespace contains module names or local function calls. A class's attributes form its own namespace. Identical names belonging to several namespaces will not affect each other in any way. Let's look at modules to better appreciate this. Two modules that define the same function with the same name can exist, but they won't confuse Python. Python sees them as unique and independent.

As soon as you run the interpreter, Python creates namespaces, but some are active at different times, including the last moments. For example, Python's built-in namespaces won't ever be deleted. An interpreter reads a module, a global namespace is attached to it, but when the interpreter closes, it disappears.

While specific namespaces are pre-defined, we can't access them from anywhere. This is because of scope. In this instance, scope refers to the section of the application we can't access directly. The last time we talked about scope, we had two scopes: globals and local. In this instance, we have three of them. The first scope is of the function that has a local namespace. The second is the module creating a global namespace. The third is the general scope that contains all pre-built namespaces.

Defining a Class

Let's look at class syntax. Below is an example:

```
class Raven:
    <myStatement1>
    <myStatement2>
```

```
<myStatement3>
```

Defining a class is somewhat similar to defining a function. Class definitions are performed before we see any results. Statements inside classes will often contain function definitions.

We use the "class" keyword followed by the name of a class when defining a class. Class names start with a capital letter. So, naming classes is different from naming variables and functions. Developers follow this as a standard, but it is not how Python itself operates. There won't be an error if you neglect to use variable naming conventions. That would be a bad idea, though because companies and other developers hate it for reasons we will not get into here.

Now, we use the class we created to build an object:

```
myObject = Raven()
print (myObject.x)
```

We've made an object called "myObject" and printed the value "x" that belongs to it.

Defining a Method

Objects can contain methods which are also called functions. Here's an example below:

```
class Man:
    def _init_ (self, name, age)
        self.name = name
        self.age = age
    def myfunction (self):
        print ("Hi, I am " + self.name)
x = Man ("Thomas", 25)
x.myfunction()
```

Notice that the "self" parameter refers to the current instance of the class. The "self" parameter is used to access any variable belonging to it. Know that "self" is not a keyword but is the crucial first parameter of functions belonging to a class.

You may have also noticed we used the function called "_init_" in this example. This function is called a constructor. Python has other constructors, and they are characterized by underscores at the beginning and end of the line.

Basic classes and objects aren't very useful in real-world applications, but functions like the "init" may give them a meaning. The function executes when the class is initialized. It's used to assign a number of values to an object. We can also use it to assign other important operations during object creation.

Python Inheritance

Inheritance is an important programming concept. It happens when classes inherit the functionality of the parent class. The subclass is called the child class, and the parent class is called the main class. Let's look at the syntax:

```
class MainClass:
    #add functions and statements
class ChildClass (MainClass):
    #add functions and statements
```

Inheritance allows you to add or modify features in the subclass.

There are several kinds of inheritance in Python:

- Single inheritance: This is what we have done so far. It happens when there is one child class inheriting from a parent class.

- Multiple inheritance: Multiple inheritance is when you create a child class that can inherit features from more than one parent class. The syntax does not change that much; parents are separated with commas.

- Multilevel inheritance: It's when a child class has another class under it that inherits its class features. It is also referred to as the grandchild class because the child class becomes the parent of the second class and parent class because of the grandparent of the second child class.

- Hierarchical inheritance: When a parent class creates multiple subclasses, we have hierarchical inheritance.

- Hybrid inheritance: When types of inheritance are combined, we say we have hybrid inheritance.

Polymorphism

Polymorphism means having many forms. In programming, it refers to a language's ability to process objects by their class or data type. An object can redefine the method that is inherited and adapt code for the data type it will process.

Polymorphism is a somewhat advanced topic. So if you don't quite get it yet, it's okay, but let's go through an analogy to explain. Imagine you gave cash to a friend to buy you something for lunch. If you told an 11-year-old kid to do the same thing for you, they'd get on a bike and get you hamburgers and fries. But your friend might get into their car and get you a vegan sandwich and grapes. That is polymorphic: you have one goal that different objects can accomplish in different ways. Keep this in mind when we talk about the same thing but in programming speak.

Polymorphism is important for two reasons. It allows an object, depending on its parameters, to perform diverse implementations of a method. Secondly, code for one data type can be used for another related data type. Understanding this is important for mastering Python.

Another feature of polymorphism that is similar to the real world is that it gives a language the ability to pass through the class hierarchy. This means its performance is something it's used to because it learned it in the past.

Here's an analogy for you: it's like reading this book. You know how to read it because you learned how to read books when you were young. In object-oriented programming terms, you are an object that can interact with a book, turn the page, and transform letters into words with meaning. But if you can read this book, it means you can read other things as well, like a web page. They both contain words but no flipping of pages. But you can also use this to do other things, like read street signs and text messages. All of these things are possible because you learned to read books. Reading books is the base object.

In programming, this is what polymorphism means. Code written for a specific type can perform actions on a related data type.

Creating Modules

Now, you have some experience using Python modules and importing. In Python, you can write your own modules.

Writing modules is another case of reusing and repurposing code. Say you worked on a card game, and during that time, you made classes like cards and deck. When creating another card game, you may need those classes even when the game is different - classes like cards and decks.

Modules also provide program management. When programs grow, it can be hard to keep track of all parts. Modules allow you to break them up into small pieces you can easily manage. Say you're working on a commercial project, meaning you have thousands of lines of code. You can use modules to separate them into manageable packages. This means certain programs can work on certain parts while others are working on others. They wouldn't get confused about who is working on what because the program is nicely divided.

You can also share modules with friends and other programmers. You can upload them on a community forum or email them. Anyone who has a use for them will import them into their projects.

Writing a Module

We will make a module to use in a simple game. Writing modules is done the same way as writing any other program, but you plan it. You need to consider the functions and classes you will need. Then you place them in a file that can be imported to other projects.

Let's make a module called "game." We will create a class and two functions that perform common tasks in games. Below is the code.

```
# game
# Example of writing a custom module
class Player(object):
""" A basic player. """
def __init__(self, name, score = 0):
self.name = name
self.score = score
```

```
def __str__(self):
rep = self.name + ":\t" + str(self.score)
return rep
def ask_yes_or_no(question):
    """Ask a yes or no question."""
response = None
while response not in ("y", "n"):
response = input(question).lower()
return response
def ask_number(question, low, high):
    """Ask for a number within a range."""
response = None
while response not in range(low, high):
response = int(input(question))
return response
if __name__ == "__main__":
print("This module was executed directly without importing.")
input("\n\nPress the enter key to quit.")
```

The module will be called "games" because modules take the name of their file. The code is easy to read since we have already used some of the functions in our examples. There is the "player" class that defines an object. The object has two attributes set in a constructor. We also have an "if" statement that verifies if the program is executed directly. If the check is true, the application runs directly, and if it is false, it will be an imported module.

Summary

In this chapter, we have learned about Python's object-orientated programming. We aimed to introduce you to OOP. OOP is an academic topic, so if you don't quite get it, don't be frustrated.

We have learned about classes, polymorphism, and inheritance. We also learned about modules and making your own. Making your code reusable is one of the most important things a programmer should do. So if you wrote a good function module, save it so you can use it later.

CHAPTER 8:

Exceptions

No matter how skilled we are or how much we prepare, projects never go as smoothly as we would want. As a programmer, you need to mentally prepare for this.

Exceptions are errors that show up when there is a problem with your code. You will often have to fix these errors. Some developers' entire job is fixing these errors. That is why we will focus on how to fix errors in this chapter.

When Things Go Haywire

Smaller, simple programs never display strange behavior because the code is simple. Take the "Hello World" application we started with. It's so easy that you know if you run it once, it will always run. But the more lines of code you write and more advanced your techniques, the more your chances of encountering exceptions and errors increase. Looking at your code can be deceiving. It might not always work as intended.

Here's an example. What if your application's configuration file has the wrong settings? Or what happens if it is missing? Big programs with thousands of lines will at some point contain or update data that is no longer useful. But in some instances, the code and the data are fine, but your application depends on connections to the web server to collect information, but that connection is dead. In some cases, the error is an artifact of the design, and can be ignored because it doesn't affect what your program needs to do.

Python only notifies you when it is prevented from performing the normal flow of instructions. So, you get an exception. Now, you might want to go into your code and add additional lines to handle the exception. But this is a bad strategy. Python has an exception handling methodology that is easy to follow, and its exception handling tools are the most useful.

Basic Exceptions

To demonstrate, we will start with basic errors, like dividing by zero. It's the type of errc wouldn't make, but it will trigger an exception, and we are interested in learning h. handle those. Type the following code:

```
1 / 0
Traceback (most recent call last):
File "<stdin>", line 1, in <module>
ZeroDivisionError: int division or modulo by zero
```

In an earlier chapter, we encountered an error that gave us a report like this one. Let's look at the operation. Division always requires a dividend and a divisor. Python goes through several verifications to make sure that those standards are met. It checks whether both arguments are numbers and whether the divisor is not zero. Only when these checks are performed can the operation be performed. If the operation does not meet those standards, an exception describing the error is generated. In programming, we say the operation raised an exception.

The word "raised" is descriptive because it refers to the hierarchical order. So the first function calls the second function containing division by zero. The second function deals with the exception, so it raised it with the first function. In the end, it can't be handled altogether, so it is raised with you. The exception is easy to understand. The report it produces is called a traceback.

In some programming languages, exceptions are not raised; they are thrown or caught. So it is thrown to the second function, which fails to catch it and brings it to the first function. But it still refers to the same thing.

One of the easiest ways to deal with the exception is by using the "try" statement in your script. "Try" looks for errors, and an except block handles them. Below is an example of this:

```
print(x)
```

"X" is undefined, meaning it will cause an error. Without a try statement, the program will crash. Now let's handle the exception:

```
try:
    print (x)
except:
    print ("An exception occurred")
```

It is also possible to define multiple exception statements to catch as many errors as you want. Here's an example:

```
try:
    print (x)
except NameError:
    print ("There is no definition for variable x")
except:
    print ("Something else went wrong")
```

If you get a NameError exception, the program prints the first message, and other errors will print the second message.

You can also use the "else" keyword to specify the code you want executed if there aren't errors. Here is an example:

```
try:
    print ("Hello World")
except:
    print ("An error occurred")
else:
    print ("Everything is fine")
```

Exceptions Classes

Python has several exception classes that tell programmers what went wrong with the code. They are subclasses of the main exception class "BaseException," meaning every exception emanates from this class.

We are going to raise several exceptions to find out what features they inherit. We will do this by handling exceptions with an array, so we can store them and inspect them. Here's the code below:

```
store = []
# Create a number of different exceptions and handle them
try: {}["foo"]
except KeyError as e: store.append(e)
try: 1 / 0
except ZeroDivisionError as e: store.append(e)
try: "".bar()
except AttributeError as e: store.append(e)
# Loop through the errors and print the class ladder
for exception_object in store:
ec = exception_object.__class__
print(ec.__name__)
indent = " +-"
while ec.__bases__:
# Assign ec's superclass to itself and increase
ec = ec.__bases__[0]
print(indent + ec.__name__)
indent = " " + indent
```

The result should look something like this:

```
KeyError
+-LookupError
+-Exception
+-BaseException
+-object
ZeroDivisionError
+-ArithmeticError
+-Exception
```

```
+-BaseException
+-object
AttributeError
+-Exception
+-BaseException
+-object
```

We have now retrieved every exception class hierarchy. You can find them all in the Python document library to learn more about them. In reality, you won't work with a list of exceptions next to you. You will focus on specific ones and handle them rather than try to catch every exception. While each class in Python can be found in the hierarchy, this will also include custom exceptions. You can create exceptions that can also inherit from the parent classes. We won't talk about this more as it is an advanced topic.

Assertion Error

The purpose of this error is to tell the programmer there is an error the program can't recover. They don't show typical reports, which allows you to act in some way. Assertions are like a self-check in the code. They check if the code contains impossible conditions. If they are found, the program crashes, and you will receive an assertion error. It will tell you which impossible condition caused it.

Assertion errors can warn you of bugs that need fixing. To add an assertion, you need to use the "assert" keyword. Developers place the assert statement at the beginning of the function to check input and end to check the output. When Python detects an assert statement, it analyzes the expression. If the expression returns true, the function can be performed; if false, you get the assertion error.

Here's an example of the syntax:

```
assert Expression [Arguments]
```

Assertion errors can be handled exactly like exceptions errors with "try / except" statements. Ensure you catch them, or the program will just crash.

Summary

In this chapter, we learned about basic errors, exceptions, and how to handle them. Exception handling is a good thing to have during development. We also learned about assertion errors, which can be handled the same way as exceptions.

REFERENCES

Barry, P. (2016). Headfirst Python: a brain-friendly guide. Beijing: OReilly.

Beazley, D., & Jones, B. K. (2013). *Python cookbook: recipes for mastering Python 3*. Beijing: OReilly.

Gray, W. (2019). Learn Python programming: write code from scratch in a clear & concise way, with a complete basic course. From beginners to intermediate, an hands-on project with examples to follow step by step.

Rees, J. (2019). Python programming: a practical introduction to Python programming for total beginners. The Pragmatic Bookshelf.

Ramalho, L. (2016). Fluent Python: Clear, Concise, and Effective Programming. Beijing: OReilly.

Lutz, M. (2018). Learning Python: Powerful Object-Oriented Programming. Beijing: OReilly.

PYTHON

PROGRAMMING

The ultimate beginners guide
to master Python Programming step-by-step with
practical exercises

Mark Reed

TABLE OF CONTENTS

INTRODUCTION

This course introduces the core programming basics in handling algorithm development and program design with functions via the Python programming language. At the end of the course, readers will have an in depth knowledge on data and information processing techniques.

Readers will be able to use various Python features and modules to solve problems, create practical and contemporary Python projects, and explore various software development challenges.

Readers will learn how to import the random module and use it to secure data by implementing a cryptographical method to securely generate a pseudorandom number such as a password or PIN. They will also be able to use other modules such as the datetime module, time module, OS module, and OS.Path module to perform various functionalities.

In this book, readers will learn how and why socket programming is the backbone of communication. (It makes the transfer of information between different devices and platforms possible.) The reader will be able to write a Python code that allows him or her to connect to the server machine and access a web resource or connect to a client device and execute a client-server program.

He or she will also have in-depth knowledge on how communication between a client server network works and how CGI programming is applied in various chat bots, including those in Facebook and WhatsApp.

CHAPTER ONE:

Algorithm and Information Processing

Conceptual Introduction

Computers are versatile devices that perform various tasks and solve problems. You can take advantage of a computer's performance power by using programming languages to solve various problems or perform certain tasks.

In this book, we are going to use Python, a powerful and easy-to-learn programming language. Python is an object oriented programming language and provides a platform for advanced programming. By the end of this module, you will be able to use Python to analyze a problem and come up with a suitable solution to the problem.

In the context of computer science, a computer is a general purpose device that functions on a set of provided instructions and data. The instructions are executed in order to process data. Computers receive instructions in the form of inputs, process the instructions one by one, and display the results in the form of an output.

Computers focus on two interrelated concepts: Algorithms and information processing.

Algorithms

An algorithm is a set of instructions that must be followed in order to perform a particular task or to solve a certain problem. Algorithms are not only applied to computers but to other areas as well. For example, if you followed instructions to cook a particular recipe, this set of instructions is the recipe's algorithms.

A programming algorithm acts as a recipe that describes the steps required for the computer to solve a certain problem or achieve set goals. In the cooking analogy above, the recipe acts as the procedure while the ingredients used in cooking act as the inputs. When the program follows the predetermined procedure, then it produces results in the form of outputs.

A programming algorithm gives instructions on how to do something and the computer will do exactly that. Computer programmers write these instructions via a programming language, which is typically English-based, but the computers accept data in binary form. Therefore, the instructions have to be converted into a form the computers will understand (computer language).

Some programmers use pseudocode (a semi-programming language) to describe various steps of the program algorithm. Flow charts and diagrams can also be used to indicate the flow of data and the processes to be performed up to the end of the program.

Features of an Algorithm

- Contains a finite number of instructions

- Consists of well-defined instructions

- Gives detailed description of the process that eventually terminates after arriving at the desired solution to the problem.

- Solves general problems

Example: Simple algorithm example to request a user's email address through a web-based program.

Program pseudocode:

```
Step 1: Start
Step 2: Enter a variable to store the user's email address
Step 3: If the variable is empty, clear it
Step 4: Request the user to enter an email address
Step 5: The entered data is stored in the variable
Step 6: Confirm whether the entered email is a valid email
address
Step 7: Not valid? Take the user back to Step 3
Step 8: End
```

Flowchart to represent the above program

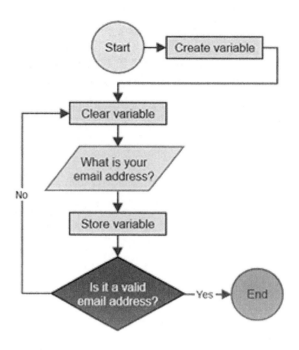

Every program procedure has a starting point and an ending point as shown above. When creating a program, you have to declare variables, which will create a memory space in the computer to store what the user types in as an input (shown in Step 2).

Once a variable is created, you have to clear it and free the memory to be used again. You don't want to have the old variable values mixed with the new content (Step 3).

The user is requested to enter his or her email address in Step 4. The email entered is stored in the variable created earlier.

In Step 6, we prompt the computer to check whether the email address entered is a valid email or not, then make a decision based on the information returned.

If the email address entered is not valid, the computer takes the user back to Step 3. Otherwise, if it's a valid email address, then the program should terminate.

Using Algorithms in Python Programming

To use the algorithm, you have to convert it from pseudocode to a programming language. Computers accept data and instructions using binary or machine language. This makes it impossible to write computer instructions directly as it will be difficult for humans to read. Therefore, to simplify the programming process, programmers in the early 1940s introduced the use of assembly languages.

Assembly languages are computer instructions easily understood by humans that correspond to the machine language. The computer can't directly understand all programs written in assembly languages, however, so translation programs were created to supplement the assembly languages and translate assembly language into machine language.

Although the introduction of the assembly language led to improvements in the machine language, it remained a low level language that required several instructions to perform even simple tasks. To improve programming tasks, high-level languages were developed to make it easy to read and write program instructions.

Python programming is a good example of a high-level language. For example, writing a simple code to add numbers in Python is shown below.

```
Sum = 15+25
```

This is a simple Python code that is easy to read and write. The high-level languages makes it easy to read and write program code.

Compilers and Interpreters

High-level languages need translators to translate instructions into machine language prior to execution. Translation is done either one line at a time (line-by-line) or by translating the whole program at once. The translated instructions are stored in another file which is then executed.

Program instructions translated and executed line-by-line are associated with compiled or interpreted languages. Python programming is an interpreted high-level language.

A compiled program uses a compiler to compile program source code to an executable binary form. The compiler has to read the program instructions first before the program executes. The high-level language is the source code, while the translated program is known as the object code. Once the program is translated, it can be executed repeatedly. No need for further translation.

An interpreted program, on the other hand, uses the interpreter to read instructions in source files and execute them. Programs using interpreters to execute instructions are less efficient and slower compared to compiled programs.

n language is more suitable for non-resource intensive programs. It allows programs loped more easily and rapidly.

.... high-level languages need to be processed first before they run.

Advantages of High-Level Languages

1.) Require less time to write the program code.

2.) Programs are short and easy to read compared to low-level languages

3.) They are portable; you can run the program in different platforms

Information Processing

Information processing is the process of describing how user data is processed. The process involves a sequence of events which consists of information input, processing, and information output.

When carrying out the instructions of an algorithm, the computer program manipulates data inputs to produce the desired outputs. An algorithm is used to describe an information processing and it represents information.

Structure of Modern Computer System

A computer system consists of hardware and computer software. The computer hardware represents the physical devices used in the execution of algorithms while the computer software is a set of instructions or algorithms that represent a program written in any high-level programming language.

Computer Hardware

A computer's hardware consists of components that communicate with each other and exchange information.

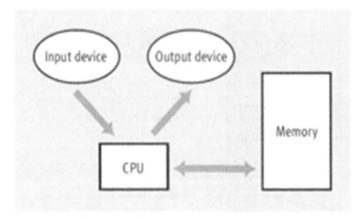

A computer can also exchange information with the external world through the use of ports

connected to other devices via a network.

A computer system consists of four components, namely:

1. Input device

An input device is any device that allows the computer to receive data from the user. The commonly used input devices include the keyboard, mouse, scanner, or microphone.

2. Processing unit

This is used to process user data. It converts the computer's raw data into meaningful information. The main processing unit is the central processing unit (CPU). There are other processing systems based on the function of the computer. For example, a graphics card system uses a graphics processing unit (GPU). GPU not only processes graphics but also processes general purpose programs.

3. Memory

This is where the processed data is stored. A computer's memory includes both the primary memory (RAM and ROM) and the secondary memory, which consists of hard drives, flash disks, DVDs, and CDs.

4. Output

An output is a device used to display information to the user. Some of common output devices include the monitor, printer, and speakers.

Central Processing unit (CPU)

The CPU is an important component in the computer system that performs instruction processing functions. The CPU is subdivided into:

- Arithmetic and logic unit (ALU): These are used to perform arithmetic calculations and comparison operations.

- Control unit: It determine the instructions to be executed. That is, it determines what is to be executed and when. It coordinates activities between the ALU, registers, and the main memory.

- Registers: They act as temporary storage areas for the processed data.

The CPU is characterized by:

- Clock speed: This is the operating speed for the CPU, and it is expressed in terms of cycles per second. The faster the clock, the faster the CPU.

- Instruction set: These are sets of instructions understood by the CPU.

Computer Memory

The computer's memory is used to store processed information for future reference. Computer memory is divided into two parts: primary memory and secondary memory.

The primary memory is the main memory connected to the CPU for processing. It is also referred to as the Random Access Memory (RAM). RAM is a temporary type of memory which loses its content once the computer is switched off.

Secondary memory is a non-volatile type of memory which is permanently available. Secondary memory is available in large sizes and is cheaper than the primary memory. A good example of the secondary memory is the hard disk.

The operating system provides a high-level interface to the secondary memory. All executed programs are directly stored into the secondary memory inform of files.

Computer Software

A software is a set of computer instructions that tells the computer what to do and how to do it. A software is a sequence of instructions which are performed to solve a particular problem. A software is divided into three parts:

- System software
- Application software
- Programming languages

System Software

System software is a collection of program instructions meant for the operation, control, and extension of the computer processing capabilities. System software consists of programs that are written in low-level languages, and they interact with the computer hardware in order to accomplish a specific task.

System software is divided into two: operating system and utility software. Translation programs like compilers, interpreters, and assemblers form part of system software.

Features of System Software

- Fast in speed
- Operate close to the system
- Not easy to design and understand
- Written using low-level language
- Difficult to manipulate

Operating system: Operating system (OS) is a program that translates computer inputs into a form computers can understand. OS acts as an interface between the various components of the computer.

The OS schedules program tasks and controls the performance of peripheral devices. It manages the computer hardware, software resources, and control services of other computer programs.

Utility software: This is a program designed to help analyze, optimize, and maintain other computer programs or resources. Examples of utility software include antivirus software, backup utility, copy utility, and dump utility.

Utility software perform tasks which ensure the smooth running of the computer system. They extend the functionality of the operating system.

Application Software

An application software is a program designed to perform a specific function. The software product is designed to satisfy a specific need. It consists of a collection of software packages that work together to achieve a common goal.

Application software rely on the OS for the running of the programs. Application software uses the operating system to make requests for services via the application program interface, or API.

Application software include:

- Accounting software: QuickBooks, Pastel, Sage, Payroll software
- Application packages: Spreadsheet, Word processor, Database management, publisher, and presentation package.
- Inventory management system, income tax software, etc.

Application software programs are written in high-level languages, and are easy to manipulate and understand.

Programming Languages

These are software programs used exclusively by computer programmers. Programming languages are high level languages that allow programmers to write program instructions to solve a specific task or build other applications.

For example, you can use programming platforms like C++, Java, PHP, Python, or other classes of languages for product development.

Computer Program

A computer program is written to solve a specific problem or to achieve a particular task. Before writing any program, you should understand the problem thoroughly so as to be in a better position to solve the problem.

Understanding the problem will help you come up with a useful plan aimed at providing a solution to the problem. This involves coming up with the inputs and outputs required. You can also structure the list of requirements in the form of diagrams like flow charts.

Once the above is done, you can come up with an algorithm to solve the problem. An algorithm is a sequence of steps as discussed earlier. Once you have come up with the algorithm, the next step is writing the program code to solve the identified problem.

Python programming is one of the most powerful object oriented programs easy to use and understand. Some parts of the algorithm will be straight forward to translate in Python.

After writing the program, check for errors. There are different types of errors you may come across when you run the program. These errors are called bugs, and the process used in tracking these errors and correcting them is known as debugging.

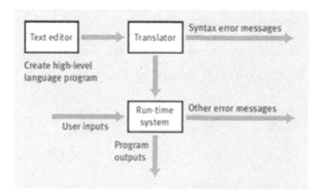

Programmers make errors when writing a program code. A Python interpreter will be able to detect these errors. Some of these errors include syntax errors, runtime errors, and semantic errors. In order to track these errors down, you have to know the differences between them.

Syntax Error

When a Python interpreter encounters an error in the program, it terminates the program and displays an error message to the user. Syntax represents the structure of a program and the rules of declaring that structure. If there is a single error, Python will quit and you will not be able to run the program.

If you're new to programming, you may spend a few days tracking syntax errors. Once you become familiar with the language, however, you will make fewer errors, and it will be easy to track them.

Runtime Error

A runtime errors occurs after running the program. That is, the error will not show up until you run the program. Runtime errors are commonly known as exceptions as they indicate something has already happened.

Semantic Errors

If a program has a semantic error, the program will run successfully and the Python interpreter will not generate the error message. The program will run up to the end but will not perform the task it was meant to do.

To correct semantic errors, you have to look at the program output and work backwards by analyzing what each output was supposed to do.

Python Basics

At this point, you already know how to set up a Python development framework from *Python programming Book One*. In this book, we will discuss how to get started using the interactive interpreter.

When you enter *python* on the command line with no parameters, it will automatically launch the Python interpreter. The Python interpreter is a text console which allows you to enter python code line by line and be interpreted on the fly.

Python Interactive Shell

While the Python interpreter executes program code line by line, the interactive shell, or python shell as commonly known, executes a single command to obtain the results. The interactive shell waits for the user's inputs, and once the user enters the input command, the program is executed immediately and the results displayed.

You can open python shell in a Windows computer by opening a command prompt, and then writing *python,* and then pressing Enter.

When you run the shell, the three greater than symbols (**>>>**) are shown. From the three symbols, you can enter single-line Python statements and get results immediately. For example, enter values to add, multiply, and divide as shown below:

Execution of Python Script

Python shell is used to execute a single statement. If you have multiple statements to be executed, you have to create a python file and write Python scripts to execute (multiple statements) instead.

For example, create a code to output the value of p. The *print ()* function will be able to output the value of p.

```
p=5;
Print (p)
```

Interpreters are essential when testing a small piece of code before using it on a complex program. This helps you know how the function works as well as ensure that the syntax of the code is correct.

An interpreter tests code snippet, explore functions, and modules. If you want to save the program, you have to write the program code into a file. All python programs are saved with an extension *.py.* You can run the code anytime using the *python* command followed by the file name as the parameter.

```
Python example.py
```

Chapter Summary

Algorithms and information processing are the fundamental components of computer science. Programmers use these components to come up with program instructions aimed at solving various problems. Software provides a platform where different algorithms can run on a general-purpose hardware device. This chapter discussed:

- How to write a program algorithm.

- How to use flowcharts and pseudocode to write a program.

- How compilers and interpreters work in a program.

- Python programming language is a high-level language. Interpreters translate instructions written in Python to a lower level form which is then executed on a normal computer system.

- Information processing of data using various computer system components.

- Highlights on various computer architecture devices and how each functions.

- The importance of computer software in handling the hardware components as well as the different types of softwares and examples in each.

- Python basics and the use of the Python shell, which provides a command prompt to evaluate and view Python expressions and statements.

- When the Python program is executed, it is translated to byte code.

In the next chapter you will learn about Python strings—how to use slice syntax to represent a substring, string methods, and other string manipulation techniques.

CHAPTER TWO:

Working with Python Strings

Python Strings

Python uses built-in strings assigned to variables. Strings are created by enclosing Python statements in quotes, either single (') quotes or double (") quotes. Creating a string in Python is as easy as creating variables and assigning values.

Assign a String to a Variable

Assigning strings to variables is accomplished by creating a variable, followed by an equal sign and then the string.

```
x="Hi!"
print (x)
```

A string can span multiple lines with each line separated by a backslash (\) at the end. String literals can use three double quotes or three single quotes to represent multiple lines of text.

Strings are immutable. That is, once you create strings in Python, you can't change them. Therefore, you have to create new strings to represent computed values. For example, ('Hello' + 'World') has two strings, 'Hello' and 'World', which are used to build a new string 'HelloWorld'.

Accessing Characters in a String

The characters in a string are accessed with the standard [] syntax just like in arrays. Python uses zero indexing to initialize the string. If the string index is out of bounds, an error is generated. Python stops executions if it can't tell what to do, in which case it sends an error message.

To extract characters from the string, enter the string name followed by the index number. For example, to retrieve character 'e' from string 'hello', you write hello[1]. The *len(string)* function returns the string length.

The [] syntax and len() function works in any sequence in strings or lists. Python uses the '+' operator to concatenate two strings.

Example:

```
a="Hello"
print a[3]
print len(a)
print a + 'there'
```

// Output

```
1        — l is the 3rd letter 0, 1, 2,
5        — ie 5 letters in hello.
```

Hello there

In some cases, the '+' operator doesn't convert numbers into string type. To do so, use the *str()* function that converts values to string form so as to combine them with other strings.

Example:

```
pi=3.14
confirm= 'the value of pi is' + str(pi)
```

// Output

```
yes
```

String Slicing

The slice syntax is a great way to return sub-parts of a string sequence. If you want to return a range of characters, you can use the slice syntax. This allows you to specify the start index and the end index separated by a colon.

To return part of a string in 'Hello World', write:

```
x='Hello'
Print (x[1:4]
//output
'ell'
```

In this case, the characters start at index 1 and extend to others characters but doesn't include the index 4.

87

x[1:] will return 'ello' – it omits the index defaults at the end (or beginning for x[:4]) of the string.

x[:] will return 'Hello' – since no string index is specified, the code returns the whole string (this is commonly used when you want to copy the entire string or list).

x[2:100] will return 'llo'. If you're working with a big index (in this case 100), it will be truncated down to a string length.

Negative Indexing

You can use negative indexing to write a slice syntax from the end of the string. The x[-1] is the last char 'o' and so on.

x[-1] returns 'o' – last character

x[-4] returns 'e' – the fourth character from the end.

x[:-3] returns 'He' – represents characters from the start of the string but doesn't include the last 3 characters.

x[-3:] returns 'llo' – represents characters starting with the third character from the end of the string and extends up to the end of the string.

Note: Python doesn't have any separate scalar 'char' type. If you have a string x[10], Python will return string_length-1 characters. The operators ==, <=, or >= all works the same way. That is, for any index n, the *x[:n] +x[n:]==x*. This also applies to the negative indexing, -n. The x[:n] and x[n:] partition a Python string into two, thus conserving all the characters.

String Methods

Python has built-in functions or methods that work well with strings. The string method runs 'on' an object. If a created variable is a string, then the *lower ()* or *upper()* functions run on the string object and return the results. The concept of running methods on objects is why Python is considered an object oriented programming language.

Some of these string methods include:

- *Strip()* which is used to eliminate the white spaces from the beginning or the end of a string.

- *Lower()* and *upper ()* methods returns the string in lower case and upper respectively.

- *Startswith(other)* and *endswith(other)* methods measure the start and end of the string.

- *Isalpha(), isspace(),* and i*sdigit()* are used to test whether the string characters belong to a certain class character.

- *Find(other)* is used to search for a particular string within the created variable and return the first index where it begins or a -1 if it's found.

- *Join(list)* is used to join together elements in a given list using the string as the delimiter. For example, join('xxx', 'yyy', 'zzz') -> ['xxx', 'yyy', 'zzz'].

- *Split('delim')* returns substring list separated by a given delimiter. Delimiter in this case acts as text and not a regular expression that is, 'xxx,yyy,zzz.split('.') –> ['xxx', 'yyy', 'zzz']. The *split()* with no arguments splits characters with white spaces.

- *Replace('old', 'new')* returns a string where the old string characters are replaced with new characters.

- *Format()* is used to format specified values within a string.

- *Count()* returns the number of times a certain character occurs in the string.

Example 1:

```
x=Hello World!
Print (x.lower())
```

This code returns the string in lowercase letters.

Example 2:

```
x=Hello World!
Print (x.replace('H', 'M'))
```

When you run the code, the 'Hello' string will be replaced with 'Mello'.

Check String

Check string is used to find out whether a certain character is present in a string. It uses the keyword *in* and *not in* to check.

Example:

```
txt= "Welcome to Python programming for advanced users"
x="ing" in txt
print(x)
```

To check if the phrase "ing" is not in the text:

89

```
txt= "Welcome to Python programming for advanced users"
x="ing" not in txt
print(x)
```

Special String Operators

Strings can be manipulated using one of the following operators.

Operator	Description	Example
+	Concatenation - Adds values on either side of the operator	a + b will give HelloPython
*	Repetition - Creates new strings, concatenating multiple copies of the same string	a*2 will give -HelloHello
[]	Slice - Gives the character from the given index	a[1] will give e
[:]	Range Slice - Gives the characters from the given range	a[1:4] will give ell
in	Membership - Returns true if a character exists in the given string	H in a will give 1
not in	Membership - Returns true if a character does not exist in the given string	M not in a will give 1
r/R	Raw String - Suppresses actual meaning of Escape characters. The syntax for raw strings is exactly the same as for normal strings with the exception of the raw string operator, the letter "r," which precedes the quotation marks. The "r" can be lowercase (r) or uppercase (R) and must be placed immediately preceding the first quote mark.	print r'\n' prints \n and print R'\n'prints \n

String Formatting Operator (%)

Python consists of the string formatting operator %. The % operator is a unique string feature that uses functions from the C language family's printf() function. Python accepts a printf-type string format with %d for integer values, %s for string, and %f for floating point numbers on the left and matching values on the right in a tuple. A tuple consists of values grouped within parentheses and separated by commas.

Example:

```
Print ("My name is %s and my weight is %d kg!" %('Faith', 50))
```

When the above code is executed, it will display:

My name is Faith and my weight is 50kg!

The list below is a set of samples that can be used together with the % operator.

Format Symbol	Conversion
%c	character
%s	string conversion via str() prior to formatting
%i	signed decimal integer
%d	signed decimal integer
%u	unsigned decimal integer
%o	octal integer
%x	hexadecimal integer (lowercase letters)
%X	hexadecimal integer (UPPERcase letters)
%e	exponential notation (with lowercase 'e')
%E	exponential notation (with UPPERcase 'E')
%f	floating point real number
%g	the shorter of %f and %e
%G	the shorter of %f and %E

Other supported samples include:

Symbol	Functionality
*	argument specifies width or precision
-	left justification
+	display the sign
<sp>	leave a blank space before a positive number
#	add the octal leading zero ('0') or hexadecimal leading '0x' or '0X', depending on whether 'x' or 'X' were used.
0	pad from left with zeros (instead of spaces)
%	'%%' leaves you with a single literal '%'
(var)	mapping variable (dictionary arguments)
m.n.	m is the minimum total width and n is the number of digits to display after the decimal point (if appl.)

Unicode String

Normal Python strings are stored using the 8-bit ASCII code. Unicode strings are stored using the 16-bit Unicode. This enables the string to accommodate a varied set of characters.

Chapter Summary

In this chapter, you learned:

- How to create strings in python

- How to access characters in a string

- How to use slicing feature to return sub-parts of a string

91

- How to apply various methods to manipulate strings like *isalpha(), isspace(), isdigit(), strip(),* and *find()* among other methods.

- How to format strings using the % operator.

In the next chapter you will learn about data sequences, basic list operators, and working with dictionaries and sets.

CHAPTER THREE:

Data Sequences, Dictionaries, and Sets

Python Sequence

A sequence is a built-in data type that consists of a series of values bound together by a container. It enables storage of multiple values in an organized and efficient manner. All streams created in Python form a sequence.

The order in which the objects are organized is similar to the order in content is retrieved from the objects.

Types of sequences include:

- String
- List
- Tuple
- Xrange objects
- Unicode
- Buffers
- Byte arrays

Strings

In the previous chapter, we covered strings in which an array element or string character is accessed with square brackets or by using the subscript operator. The arrays use indexes which are numbered from 0 to n-1, where n is the number of characters in the variable.

Example:

```
>>>"Tuple" [0]
```

```
Output 'T'
>>> "Tuple" [1]
Output 'u'
>>> "Tuple" [2]
Output 'p'
>>> "Tuple" [3]
Output 'l'
>>> "Tuple" [4]
Output 'e'
```

You can also create negative indexes by counting the string from the end.

You can declare an empty string using the str() function. For example:

```
>>>type (varname)
>>>varname=str()
>>>varname
```

Lists

A list is a group of values arranged in a specific order. It acts as a container that holds various objects in this particular order. The list type is essential for the implementation of sequence protocol. It also makes it easy to add and remove objects from a sequence.

The list elements are enclosed in square brackets. For example, you can create an empty list that is initiated as follows:

```
>>>demo= []
```

You can pass values to the list. Use commas to separate the values.

```
>>>demo ["book", "pen", "10"]
```

In this case, the list hold values of different data types. The above example holds strings "book" and "pen" as well as the number 10.

Just like string characters, the items in a list are accessed by the use of indexes starting at 0 up to n-1. If you want to access a specific item in the list, you can refer to it by using the list name followed by the item's number inside the square brackets.

```
>>> demo ["book", "pen", "10"]
>>>demo [0]
Output "book"
>>> demo [1]
Output "pen"
>>>demo [2]
Output "10"
```

If you use negative numbers, it will count backwards:

```
>>>demo [-1]
```

```
10
>>>demo [-2]
"pen"
>>>demo [-3]
"book"
```

Unlike other programming languages, Python uses the same syntax and function name to execute sequential data. For example, you can use the *len()* function to determine the length of the string, list, or tuple. It returns the number of items in the array.

Example 1:

```
>>> len(demo)
3
```

Example 2:

```
>>>subjects= ["English", "Maths", "Chemistry", "Biology"]
>>>len(subjects)
```

// output

```
4
```

Just like in strings, lists can also be sliced.

```
>>>demo [1:]
['pen', 10]
>>>demo [:-1]
['book', 'pen']
```

You can also add more items to the list by using the *append()* function, although there are various ways to add more items to a list:

```
>>>demo.append (20)
>>>demo ['book', 'pen', 10, 20]
```

If you specify the index outside the range, the code will generate an error message. Therefore, all items should be added inside the range. Alternatively, you can use *insert()* if you want to add items or elements in a particular index.

```
>>>demo.insert (1, 'and')
>>> demo ['book', 'and', 'pen', 10, 20]
```

Items can be deleted from the list using the *del()* function.

```
>>> demo ['book', 'and', 'pen', 10, 20]
>>> del demo [1]
>>>demo ['book', 'pen', 10, 20]
```

In this example, the *del ()* function deletes the string 'and' from the list. The list then re-orders itself to ensure there is no space left between the items.

Lists also portray an unusual characteristic in that, if you have two items in the list: x and y, then set y to x and change the value of x, y will change automatically as well.

```
>>>x=[5,6,7, 8]
>>>y=x
>>>del x[3]
>>>print x [3, 4, 5]
>>>print y [3, 4, 5]
```

Properties of a List

- They're represented in an ordered manner
- They have arbitrary objects
- List elements can be changed hence, they're mutable
- They have variable size
- Lists use index to access elements in the list (kept in order)

Tuples

Tuples works the same as list, except they are immutable. If you have a set of tuples, you can't change it. That is, you can't add or delete elements or change them once created. Tuple elements are enclosed in parentheses instead of square brackets, and they use the same rules of indexes as in lists.

Advantages of using tuples:

- They're faster when compared to list execution
- Prevents any accidental changes to the data. If you have data that doesn't require changes, use tuples instead of lists.
- Used as keys in a data dictionary. This is one of the major benefits of using tuples compared to the use of lists.

Tuples are declared as follows:

```
>>>tup= ("tuples", "can't", "be", "changed")
```

Bytes Object _immutable_

This is a sequence of integer number elements with bytes objects in a range of 0 to 255. These numbers correspond to the ASCII characters and printed as that.

Bytes Arrays

A byte array is the same as byte object except that it is mutable. The byte array returns an array of a particular byte size.

```
>>>x=bytearray(5)
>>>x
Bytearray(y'\x00\x00\x00\x00\x00')
To change byte array values:
>>>x=bytearray([4,5,6,7,8])
>>>x
Bytearray(b'\x04\x05\x06\x07\x08')
```

Python Sequence Operations

These are operations carried on a sequence. They include:

Concatenation

To combine two sequences is as easy as adding two numbers. You can combine lists or strings together. For example:

```
>>>fname= "Robert"
>>>lname="Mogare"
>>>name= fname + " " + lname
>>>print (name)
```

The augmented assignment operator += can also work well in sequences.

```
a+=b is syntactically equivalent to a=a+b
```

This is syntactically the same but the implementation of the two is different. In a+=b, the left side is only evaluated once. The += operator is used on mutable objects as an optimization.

Repetitions

In the examples above, we have used '+' operator for sequences. You can also use '*' operator to point to values. The '*' represent a sequence or an integer value. For example, a*n or n*a represent an object that concatenate n-times.

```
abc*4
```

is concatenated to

```
abc + abc + abc + abc
```

Membership

This is used to check whether a certain element is included in the string or not. That is, whether an element is a member of the sequence. It uses the 'in' or 'not in' operator.

```
>>>'ten' in 'concatenated'
True
>>>' t' not in concatenated
False
```

Slicing

When you want only a part of the sequence and not the entire string, you use the slicing operator.

```
>>> 'Slicing' [1:4]
'lic'
```

The slice operator allow you to extract a specific part of the string by using the index (the start and the end index with the index numbers separated by a colon).

Python Sequence Functions

Len()

The len() function is an essential function used in passing a sequence. The function returns the length of a python sequence. 8 letters

```
>>>len (sequence)
8
```

Min () and Max ()

The *min()* and *max()* functions return the lowest value and the highest value in a Python sequence.

```
>>> min(1,2,3)
'1'
>>>max (1,2,3)
'3'
```

The comparison of numbers is based on the ASCII values.

Python Index ()

This is a Python sequence method that returns the index on the first occurrence of a value.

```
>>> World.index('r')
2
```

Python Count()

The count () function returns the number of times a value occurs in a string.

```
>>>banana.index('an')
2
>>>sequence.index('e')
```

3

Python Collections

Unlike the sequences, Python collections do not have a deterministic order. When dealing with collections, the ordering of items is arbitrary and they have a physical order.

Data dictionaries and sets are containers to sequential data.

Python Sets

A set is a Python element that holds a sequence of data values. It consists of a group of items that do not hold duplicates. Sets are arranged in a sequential manner but do not support indexing.

Creating a Python Set

A set is declared by typing a sequence of values separated by commas inside curly braces, then assigning the values to a python variable.

They are declared in two ways: Assigning to Python variables and using the set() function.

Assigning to Python variable:

```
>>> num1 ={3,2,1,2}
>>>num1
1,2,3
```

Using the set() function:

```
>>> num1= set([3,2,1])
>>>num1
1,2,3
```

>>>num1= set () creates a set with an empty object. If you create an empty set, it creates an empty dictionary.

Python sets do not support indexing. Therefore, you have to access the entire set at once. From the above example, you can access the entire set at once.

```
>>>num1
{1,2,3}
```

When you call variable num1, the elements are reordered and represented in an ascending order. Since sets don't support indexing, you can't use slicing operator on them. You also can't delete a set element using indexing. If you want to delete an element from the list, you have to call the *discard()* or *remove ()* method. Each method accepts the item to be deleted as an argument.

```
>>> num1= set([3,2,1])
```

```
>>>num1.discard (2)
>>>num1
{1,3}
>>>num1.remove(1)
>>>num1
{2,3}
```

The two methods achieve the same results but work differently. If you delete an element that doesn't exist in the dictionary, the *discard()* method ignores it while the *remove()* returns a KeyError message.

The Pop () Method

You can call the *pop()* method in sets to pop out arbitrary items. The method doesn't take an argument since it doesn't support indexing and prints out the item that was popped.

```
>>>num1.pop ()
1
```

Updating a Set

Sets are mutable but do not have mutable items like lists. As we have seen, you can't reassign a set using indexes. Therefore, to update the set, you can use the *add()* and *update()* methods.

Add ()

The *add ()* function accepts the argument to be added to the set.

```
>>>values= {2, 3, 5, 5.5}
>>>values.add (6.5)
>>>values
{2, 3, 5, 5.5, 6.5}
```

If you add an already existing item in the set, the set will remain the same. The new added item will not be reflected in the set.

Update ()

The *update ()* method adds multiple items into the set. It allows you to pass several arguments into the set at once.

```
>>>values.update ([6, 7, 8, 2, 8.2])
{2, 3, 5, 5.5, 6, 7, 8, 8.2 }
```

Function Used on Sets

Sets use functions to perform a certain action or operation and return a value. The commonly used functions in sets include:

1. *Len ()*

The *len()* function returns the number of elements in a set.

```
>>>len (days)
7
```

2. *Max ()*

This function returns the highest value in a group of elements.

```
>>>max ({2, 3, 5, 4, 6})
6
```

You can also use max () on strings. For example,

```
>>>days = ({'Mon', 'Tue', 'Wed', 'Thu', 'Fri', 'Sat', 'Sun'})
>>>max (days)
wed
```

This function returns Wednesday as the maximum item as it uses ASCII values and looks at the alphabet for each day, M T W T F S T, with letter W being the highest value. Thus, the code returns Wednesday as the highest value in the set of days

3. *Min()*

The min () indicates the lowest value in a set. To get the lowest value is a set of days use:-

```
>>>min (days)
Fri
```

Letter F is the lowest ASCII Value in the set.

4. *Sum()*

The *sum ()* function is used to add numbers together. It performs arithmetic sum in a set and returns a value.

```
>>>sum ({2, 3, 5})
10
```

The *sum ()* function cannot be applied on a string.

5. *All()*

This function returns true if the values in the set have a Boolean expression with a true value. Otherwise, it will return false.

```
>>>all (days)
True
```

6. *Sorted()*

The function sorts a number of items in a set of lists. The items are sorted in ascending order without modifying the original values.

```
>>>values = {1, 2, 4, 7, 6, 5.2, 8, 9}
>>>sorted (values)
[1, 2, 4, 5.2, 6, 7, 8, 9]
```

Methods on Sets

Set methods are used to alter a set unlike functions, which perform actions on sets. Methods perform a sequence on any operation on a set. The methods are called on a set and they include:

1. *Union()*

This method is used to perform union operation on two or more sets. It returns the items in all the sets. For example:

```
>>>num1, num2, num3 = {2, 3, 4}, {4, 5, 6}, {6, 7, 8}
>>>num1.union (num2, num3)
[2, 3, 4, 5, 6, 7, 8]
```

The above method didn't alter the sets. Therefore, not all methods called will alter the set.

2. *Intersection()*

This method accepts an argument in the set and then returns all common items in the selected set.

```
>>> num2.intersection (num1)
4
>>>num2.intersection (num1, num3)
Set ()
```

Intersecting the three sets returned an empty set since there is nothing common in the three sets.

3. *Difference()*

This method is used to return the difference between two or more sets. It returns values in the form of a set.

```
>>>num1.difference (num 2)
{2,3}
```

4. *Symmetric_difference ()*

This returns all elements which are unique to each set.

```
>>>num1.symmetric_difference (num2)
{2, 3 5, 6}
```

102

2 and 3 are available in num1 while 5 and 6 are in num2. It omitted 4 because is available on both sets.

5. *Intersection_update ()*

This function returns an item which is common to both sets. The method doesn't update the set on which a call is placed.

```
>>>num1.intersection_update (num2)
>>>num 1
{4}
```

6. *Copy()*

This method is used to create a shallow copy of the set

```
>>>num4= num1. Copy()
>>>num1, num4
{2, 3, 4}, {2, 3, 4}
```

7. *Isdisjoint()*

If two sets have a null intersection, then this method will return true.

```
>>> {2, 3, 4}.isdisjoint({5, 6, 8})
True
```

The isdisjoint () only accepts one set of arguments. If you have more than one set, it will return an error.

8. *Issubset ()*

It returns true if a particular set in an arguments contain another set.

```
>>> {4, 5}. Issubset ({4, 5, 6})
True
>>> {1, 3} .issubset ({1, 3})
True
```

9. *Issuperset()*

Just like issubset (), issuperset () returns true if one set has arguments in the set.

```
>>> {2, 3, 4}.issuperset({1,2})
False
>>> {2, 3, 4}.issuperset ({2})
True
```

Python Boolean

Booleans are a type of data that returns a value as either true or false. Set methods like *isalpha* *(), issubset (),* and *issuperset ()* return a Boolean value true or false.

Declare boolean data types as you would declare a normal integer.

```
>>>days= True
```

If you add quotes to the value, it becomes a string instead of Boolean.

The Bool () Function

The *bool ()* function is used to convert a value into Boolean type.

```
>>>bool ('data')
True
>>>bool ([])
False
```

Different data values have different Boolean values equivalent to them. You can use the *bool () set* function to find out these values. For example, the Boolean value for 0 is false while the Boolean value for 1 is true. Any value greater than 0 like 0.00001 has a true Boolean value.

```
>>>bool (0)
False
>>>bool (0.0000001)
True
```

A string with values has a true Boolean value while an empty string has a false Boolean value.

```
>>>bool (' ')
True
>>>bool ('')
False
```

An empty construct has a false Boolean value while a non-empty construct has a true Boolean value.

```
>>>bool (())
False
>>>bool ((2, 5, 3))
True
```

Boolean Operations

You can perform arithmetic calculations on sets, in which a 0 value returns false and a 1 returns true, and then apply arithmetic operators to them. Some of these arithmetic operators include:

1. *Addition*

This is used to add two or more Boolean expressions.

```
>>> True +False //equivalent to 1+0
1
```

```
>>>True+True   //equivalent to 1+1
2
>>> False+False  //0+0
0
>>>False+True //0+1
1
```

2. Subtraction and multiplication

You can also adopt the same mechanism when performing subtraction and multiplication operations.

```
>>>False – True   //0-1
-1
```

3. Division

When you divide Boolean numbers, it results in a floating number value.

```
>>>False/True
0.0
>>>True/False
Zero Division error.
```

This returns an error message since you can't divide a value by zero.

4. Modulus, exponential and floor division.

All rules applied in addition, multiplication, and division also apply to modulus operators as well as in exponential and floor division operations.

```
>>> False % True
>>>True ** False
1
>>>False **False
1
>>False // True    //equivalent to 0//1
```

Relational Operators

The following relational operators are also applied to Boolean values.

Operator	Description
>	Greater than
>=	Greater than or equal to

<	Less than
<=	Less than or equal to
!=	Not equal to
==	Equal to

Example:

```
>>>0<=1
True
 0 is less than or equal to 1.
>>>false>true
False
```

The value of false is 0 while the value of true is 1. As 0 is not greater than 1, False is returned.

Bitwise Operator

Bitwise operators use bit-by-bit operation. Assume you have OR code with 2(010) bits and 2(020) bits. This will result in 4(030) bits.

```
>>>2/3
5
```

Common bitwise operators used in Boolean expressions include:

1. *Bitwise and (&)*

This operator only returns true if both Boolean expressions are true.

```
>>> True & False
False
>>> True & True
True
```

2. *Bitwise or (|)*

This operator only returns a false value if both of the values are false.

```
>>> False |True
True
```

3. *Bitwise XOR (^)*

This operator returns a true value if one of the values is true and the other value is false. It returns false if the two values are the same

```
>>> True ∧ True
False
>>> True ∧ False
True
```

4. Binary 1's complement

The binary 1's complement calculates a value to either true indicated by 1 or false indicated by 0.

Python Dictionary

A dictionary holds real, mutable values. A dictionary allows you to add, change, or remove elements in the same manner as in lists, although numbers do not bind elements in the dictionary.

Each element in a dictionary has a key and a value in a (key:value) pair. If you call the key, it returns the corresponding value linked to tthathe key. Lists represents a unique type of dictionary in which the key in each element is a number in a particular order.

Dictionaries are optimized to retrieve data elements using keys. Data values can be of any data type within the dictionary.

Dictionary Definition and Declaration

You can create a dictionary using the key and placing the values inside the curly braces ({}) separated by a colon. It can also be created using the built-in *dict()* function. You can create an empty dictionary by using the curly braces only.

```
>>>sample_dict= {'name':1, 'DOB': 2} # using integer keys
>>>Sample_dict= dict({1: 'name', 2: 'DOB'})  # using dict()
>>>Sample_dict = {} # empty dictionary
>>>sample_dict ={'name': 'DOB', 1: [3, 5, 7]  # Dictionary with
mixed keys
>>>sample_dict = dict([(1, 'name'), (2, 'DOB')]) # Dictionary
with each of the items as a pair.
```

Adding Values to a Dictionary

Adding values to a dictionary can be done in various ways. You can add one value at a time to the dictionary by assigning the value to be used to the dictionary key. For example, Sample-_dict [key] = value. You can add more items to the dictionary using the *update()* built-in method. You can also update the dictionary using nested values.

When updating a dictionary with a pre-existing key, the key is updated with the new value. Otherwise, a new key is created to store the value.

Example: Program to add values to dictionary

```
# create an empty dictionary
New_dict = {}
Print ('This is an empty dictionary:  ')
print (new_dict)

 #adding values one at a time
new_dict [0]= 'Adding'
new_dict [1]= 'values'
new_dict [2]= 'to'
new_dict [3]= 'dictionary'
print ('\nUpdating dictionary with 4 elements: ')
print (new_dict)
#adding a set of values using a single key
new_dict['value_set'] =3, 5, 6
print ('\nAdding set of values to the dictionary: ')
print (new_dict)

#Using existing key value to update dictionary
new_dict[0]= 'Update'
print ('\nUpdate dictionary key value: ')
print (new_dict)

# updating dictionary with nested key elements
new_dict [7]= {'Nested' :{'1' : 'Data', '2': 'elements'}}
print ('\n Adding a nested key to the dictionary: ')
print (new_dict)
```

// Output

```
This is an empty dictionary:
{}

Updating dictionary with 4 elements:
{0: 'Adding', 1: 'values', 2: 'to', 3: 'dictionary'}

Adding set of values to the dictionary:
{0: 'Adding', 1: 'values', 2: 'to', 3: 'dictionary',
'value_set': (3, 5, 6)}

Update dictionary key value:
{0: 'Update', 1: 'values', 2: 'to', 3: 'dictionary',
'value_set': (3, 5, 6)}

Adding a nested key to the dictionary:
{0: 'Update', 1: 'values', 2: 'to', 3: 'dictionary',
'value_set': (3, 5, 6), 7: {'Nested': {'1': 'Data', '2':
'elements'}}}
```

Accessing Elements from a Dictionary

To access items in the dictionary, you have to call the key name to the dictionary. The key item is put inside the square brackets. You can also use the *get()* function to access the contents of the dictionary.

108

Example: Access dictionary elements

```
#create new dictionary
new_dict= {1: 'New', 2: 'Dictionary', 3: 'Elements'}

#accessing elements using key
print ('\nAccessing dictionary elements with a key: ')
print (new_dict ['1'])

#accessing elements using get () method
print ('\nAccessing dictionary elements using the get: ')
print (new_dict.get(2))
```

// Output

```
Accessing dictionary elements with a key:
New

Accessing dictionary elements using the get:
Dictionary
```

Removing Elements from a Dictionary

You can delete elements from the dictionary using the *del* keyword. This keyword deletes specific data values from the dictionary or the entire content. Functions like *pop()* and *popitem()* delete specific data elements or arbitrary elements from the dictionary.

You can also delete all elements at once using the *clear()* function. In the case of nested values, you can delete specific nested data elements using the *del* keyword supplied with the specific nested key to be deleted.

Note: using *del dict* deletes the entire dictionary, and if you try to print it, it will generate an error.

Example: Deleting elements from a dictionary

```
#Creating a dictionary:
New_dict= {1: 'welcome', 2: 'to', 3: 'Python', 4: 'Programming',
'x':{5: 'containers', 6: 'in', 7: 'sequence'},
'y':{5: 'dictionary', 6: 'containers'}}
print ('\nDictionary creation: ')
print (new_dict)

#delete elements using the key value
del new_dict [4]
print ('\nDeleting a specific key element: ')
print (new_dict)
 #deleting nested elements
del new_dict ['y'][5]
print ('\nDeleting nested key element from dictionary: ')
print (new_dict)
```

```
# deleting using pop ()
new_dict.pop (1)
print ('\nDeleting items using pop: ')
print (new_dict)

#delete items using arbitrary key value (('y', {6:
'containers'}))
new_dict.popitem()
print ('\nPopping out arbitrary key value pair: ')
print (new_dict)

#delete the whole dictionary
new_dict.clear ()
print ('Deleting the entire dictionary: ')
print (new_dict)

// Output
Dictionary creation
{1: 'Welcome', 2: 'to', 3: 'Python', 4: 'Programming', 'x': {5:
'containers', 6: 'in', 7: 'sequence'}, 'y': {5: 'dictionary', 6:
'containers'}}

Deleting a specific key element:
{1: 'Welcome', 2: 'to', 3: 'Python', 'x': {5: 'containers', 6:
'in', 7: 'sequence'}, 'y': {5: 'dictionary', 6: 'containers'}}

Deleting nested key element from dictionary:
{1: 'Welcome', 2: 'to', 3: 'Python', 'x': {5: 'containers', 6:
'in', 7: 'sequence'}, 'y': {6: 'containers'}}

Deleting items using pop:
{2: 'to', 3: 'Python', 'x': {5: 'containers', 6: 'in', 7:
'sequence'}, 'y': {6: 'containers'}}

Popping out arbitrary key value pair:
{2: 'to', 3: 'Python', 'x': {5: 'containers', 6: 'in', 7:
'sequence'}}

Deleting the entire dictionary
{}
```

Dictionary Built-In Methods

Method	Description
clear()	Removes all the elements from the dictionary
copy()	Returns a copy of the dictionary
fromkeys()	Returns a dictionary with the specified keys and values
get()	Returns the value of the specified key
items()	Returns a list containing a tuple for each key value pair
keys()	Returns a list containing the dictionary's keys
pop()	Removes the element with the specified key
popitem()	Removes the last inserted key-value pair
setdefault()	Returns the value of the specified key. If the key does not exist: insert the key, with the specified value
update()	Updates the dictionary with the specified key-value pairs
values()	Returns a list of all the values in the dictionary

Chapter Summary

Data sequences enable you to develop a series of objects using various built-in datatypes. A sequence ensures that all data objects and values are organized in an efficient manner. In the chapter, you learned about the different components of a sequence, which includes lists, strings, tuples, and buffers among other elements. You also learned:

- How to use lists in the implementation of Python programs

- How to develop objects using various built-in data types

- Byte objects and its use of ASCII characters, including how byte arrays work to return an array of a particular byte size

- Carry out various operations carried out in Python

- Use concatenation operator to join strings

- How to create sets and use various functions in sets

- How to use Boolean expressions to return values as true or false

- Performing calculations using Booleans operators

- How to use Bitwise operators

- How to retrieve data from the dictionary or add values to the dictionary

In the next chapter you will learn about the math module in Python, as well as the random module and seeding function.

111

CHAPTER FOUR:

Math Functions in Python

Introduction

Python programming has a special predefined math module. The module library provides a variety of functions and properties or constants that help you perform mathematical tasks. Library properties and functions such as logarithmic functions, representation functions, trigonometric functions, and angle conversion functions among others have static objects.

The module defines two mathematical constants: pi and Euler's number. Python properties are accessed through *math.pi* while the functions are accessed through *math.abs (number)*.

 Pi (n) is a constant defined as the ratio between a circle's circumference and diameter. It has a value of 3.141592653589793. Euler's number (e) is another mathematical constant defined in the math's module. It is the base of a natural logarithm with a value of 2.718281828459045.

```
>>> import math
>>> math.pi
3.141592653589793
>>> math.e
2.718281828459045
```

Other constants include inf and nan. *Math.inf* is a math property that returns a positive infinity. It can also be used to return a negative infinity. *Math.nan* returns Not a Number as the output.

To use the math module, you have to first import it to a Python program. Math modules have functions to calculate trigonometric ratios in a specific angle. Functions like sin, cos, and tan pass angles in radians as the function arguments. We normally present angles in degree form, but the math module represents angles in the form of radians. Therefore, the module has *degrees()* and *radians()* conversion functions used to convert degrees into radians and vice versa.

Example:

```
>>> math.radians(20)
0.3490658503988659
>>> math.degrees (math.e/6)
25.957679382967953
>>> math.radians (45)
0.7853981633974483
>>> math.degrees (math.pi/4)
45.0
>>> math.cos (0.526890)
0.8643751040967125
>>> math.tan (0.583589)
0.6603101237742569
```

Python Math Functions

A Python interpreter has a wide range of built-in functions for performing various tasks. For example, the *print ()* function is used to print a particular object in a standard output device or use a text stream file.

The different classes of math functions supported by Python library include:

Numbers and Numeric Representation

Some of the functions used to represent numbers include

Sr.No.	Function & Description
1	**ceil(x)** Return the Ceiling value. It is the smallest integer, greater or equal to the number x.
2	**copysign(x, y)** It returns the number x and copy the sign of y to x.
3	**fabs(x)** Returns the absolute value of x.
4	**factorial(x)** Returns factorial of x. where x ≥ 0
5	**floor(x)** Return the Floor value. It is the largest integer, less or equal to the number x.
6	**fsum(iterable)** Find sum of the elements in an iterable object

113

7	gcd(x, y)
	Returns the Greatest Common Divisor of x and y
8	isfinite(x)
	Checks whether x is neither an infinity nor nan.
9	isinf(x)
	Checks whether x is infinity
10	isnan(x)
	Checks whether x is not a number.
11	remainder(x, y)
	Find remainder after dividing x by y.

Power and Logarithmic Functions

These functions calculate power and logarithmic tasks. They include:

Sr.No.	Function & Description
1	pow(x, y)
	Return the x to the power y value.
2	sqrt(x)
	Finds the square root of x
3	exp(x)
	Finds xe, where e = 2.718281
4	log(x[, base])
	Returns the Log of x, where base is given. The default base is e
5	log2(x)
	Returns the Log of x, where base is 2
6	log10(x)
	Returns the Log of x, where base is 10

Example:

The *math.log()* function returns the logarithm of a specific number. Natural logarithms are always calculated to the base e.

```
>>> math.log (5)
1.6094379124341003
>>> math.log10 (5)
0.6989700043360189
```

The *math.log10()* returns the logarithm to the base of 10 for a given number.

```
>>> math.sqrt(81)
9.0
```

Trigonometric and Angular Conversion Functions

These functions calculate different trigonometric functions.

Sr.No.	Function & Description
1	**sin(x)** Return the sine of x in radians
2	**cos(x)** Return the cosine of x in radians
3	**tan(x)** Return the tangent of x in radians
4	**asin(x)** This is the inverse operation of the sine, there are acos, atan also.
5	**degrees(x)** Convert angle x from radian to degrees
6	**radians(x)** Convert angle x from degrees to radian

Random Module in Python

Functions in the random module use a pseudo-random number generator tool to generate floating point numbers between 0.0 and 1.0.

```
>>> import random
>>> random.random()
0.0952389196671356
```

Random() is the basic function in the module and almost all other functions in the random module depend on it. The *random()* returns a floating point number in the range of 0.0 to 1.0.

The *random.random()* function doesn't need arguments or no arguments. To generate random integers, you can use:

- randint ()
- randrange ()
- choice()
- shuffle()
- sample()

Randint ()

Randint() is an inbuilt function in the random module, which provides access to various functions used in generating random numbers. The *randint()* function should have both start and end arguments, which must be integer type values. The syntax for this function is *randint(start,end)*.

Example:

```
>>> random.randint(2, 10)
6
>>> random.randint(25, 70)
70
>>> random.randint (30, 50)
49
```

Random.randint() returns an integer value within a range of specified integer numbers.

Errors and Exceptions

Randint () returns two types of errors: ValueError and TypeError.

ValueError: This is an error returned after passing floating point values as arguments to the function.

TypeError: The error occurs when any parameter is passed as argument to the function that is not an integer value.

Example: Program to print random numbers

```
# Generate random numbers of range 10 to 40
rm1= random.randint (10, 40)
print ('Random numbers in the range between 10 and 40 is %d'
%(rm1))

# random number for a range of negative values
rm2= random.randint (-5, -1)
print ('Random numbers between -5 and -1 is %d' %(rm2))
```

// Output

```
Random numbers in the range between 10 and 40 is 17
Random numbers between -5 and -1 is -3
Example: Program to determine a lucky draw
```

The *randint()* function can be used in a lucky draw simulation to select a random number. The user has a chance to guess the winning number and if the guess is right, he wins. Otherwise, he will lose the competition.

```
import random
from random import randint
def generator(): # function to generate a random number on each
execution
    return randint(1,10)
```

```
def rand_guess(): # function to return true or false based on
user lucky draw
    random_number = generator() # call to generator()
    guess_left = 3 # define the number of guesses the user gets
    flag = 0 # define flag variable to check the win condition
    while guess_left > 0:
        guess = int(input("Pick your number to enter the lucky
draw\n"))
        if guess == random_number:
            flag = 1 # set flag as 1 if user guesses correctly.
Then break loop
            break
        else:
            print("Wrong Guess!!")
            guess_left -= 1 # decrease number of remaining
guesses by 1
    if flag is 1: # if win condition is satisfied, then
rand_guess returns true
        return True
    else:
        return False
# Driver code
if __name__ == '__main':
    if rand_guess() is True:
        print("Congrats!! You win.")
    else:
        print("Sorry, You Lost!")
```

// Output

```
Pick your number to enter the lucky draw
8
Wrong Guess!!
Pick your number to enter the lucky draw
9
Wrong Guess!!
Pick your number to enter the lucky draw
0
Congrats!! You Win.
```

Randrange () Method

The *random.randrange ()* function returns a random element from the range given. The random element is selected from the start, stop, and step arguments. The start value is always 0 by default while the step value is 1 by default.

The step value is optional and it indicates the difference between each of the numbers in the sequence.

```
>>> import random
>>> random.randrange (2, 8)
6
>>> random.randrange (1, 15, 10)
```

117

```
11
>>> random.randrange (0, 80, 20)
20
```

Choice() Method

Random.choice () is used to return a random value selected from an empty sequence. When you use an empty sequence as argument, an IndexError is generated.

```
>>> import random
>>> random.choice([10, 20, 25, 32, 38,42])
32
>>> random.choice([5, 7, 8, 9, 11, 13])
13
>>> random.choice('user')
'r'
```

Example 2: Randomly select a city from a list

```
import random
city= ['Nairobi', 'Mombasa', 'Kisumu', 'Eldoret', 'Nakuru']
print ('Select your favorite city from the list: ',
random.choice(city))
print ('Select your favorite city from the list: ',
random.choice(city))
```

// Output

```
Select your favorite city from the list:  Nakuru
Select your favorite city from the list:  Mombasa
```

Shuffle() Method

The *random.shuffle()* function randomly reorder elements within a list.

```
>>> import random
>>> values= [12, 32, 23, 30, 45, 32, 48, 38, 50]
>>> random.shuffle(values)
>>> values
[32, 32, 30, 48, 23, 38, 12, 50, 45]
>>> random.shuffle(values)
>>> values
 [23, 45, 48, 50, 12, 38, 32, 30, 32]
```

Sample() method

The *random.sample(population, k)* method is used when you want to select several random elements from a population. This method returns a list of unique elements selected from a population. The size of the population, k, depends on the total number of elements you want to select. A population can be a set of numbers, a list, or a sequence.

Example:

```
>>> import random
>>> new_list= [2,5,7,8,10,12]
>>> print ('random.sample() ', random.sample(new_list,3))
random.sample()  [8, 7, 5]
```

Example: Program to play dice

```
#dice game
 import random
 firstplayer= 'moses'
 secondplayer= 'joseph'
 mosesscore=0
 josephscore=0
 firstdice= [2, 3, 5, 6, 7, 8]
 seconddice= [2, 3, 5, 6, 7, 8]
 def dicegame(): #players will roll the dice using the shuffle
method
          for x in range(4):
                   random.shuffle(firstdice)
                   random.shuffle(seconddice)

     choose_first_number=random.choice(firstdice)#picking a
single random number

     choose_second_number=random.choice(seconddice)
                   return choose_first_number +
choose_second_number
          print ('This is a dice game using the random
module\n')

 def dicegame(): #players will roll the dice using the shuffle
method.
         for x in range(4):
                   random.shuffle(firstdice)
                   random.shuffle(seconddice)

     choose_first_number=random.choice(firstdice)#picking a
single random number

     choose_second_number=random.choice(seconddice)
                   return choose_first_number +
choose_second_number
          print ('This is a dice game using the random
module\n')
          for x in range (3):
                   moses_toss_number=random.randint(1,70)
                   joseph_toss_number=random.randrange(1, 71,
1)

                   if(moses_toss_number>joseph_toss_number):
                           print('Moses won the toss')
                           mosesscore=dicegame()
                           josephscore=dicegame()
```

```
                          else:
                print('Joseph won the toss')
                mosesscore=dicegame()
                josephscore=dicegame()
        if(mosesscore>josephscore):
                print ('Moses won the game. Moses score
is:', mosesscore, and 'Joseph's score is:', josephscore, '\n')
                else:
                print('Joseph won the game. Joseph's
score is:', josephscore, and 'Moses score is:', mosesscore,
'\n')
```

// Output

```
Joseph won the toss
Moses won the game. Moses score is: 9 and Joseph's score is: 6

Joseph won the toss
Moses won the game. Moses score is: 11 and Joseph's score is: 9

Moses won the toss
Joseph won the game. Joseph's score is: 12 and Moses score is: 6
```

The Seed () Function in Python

Not all the random numbers generated in python are fully random. They are pseudo-random generated using a Pseudorandom Number Generator (PRNG). PRNG is an algorithm that not only generates a seemingly random number but also is used in reproducing data.

PRNG uses a software tool to generate random numbers. This tool works by getting a random number known as the seed and then using an algorithm that generates a pseudo-random sequence of bits based on the seed.

The pseudo-random generator relies on the previous generated value to perform its operation on the value. However, when you use the generator for the first time, there is no previous value stored in the memory. Therefore, the seeding pseudo-random generator generates the first previous value. The seeding value is equivalent to the generated value in any particular random generator number. If you pass the same parameters to the seed twice, it will generate the same sequence of numbers twice.

The *seed()* method initiates the pseudorandom number generator while the random module uses the seeding value as the base when generating random numbers. If the seeding value is unavailable, the current date will be used. If the same value is passed to the seed before generating a random number, then it will generate the same number. To generate a seed, use Seed([n]) where n is the random number. If omitted, then the system time will be automatically used in generating the next random number

The *seed ()* function cannot be accessed directly; therefore, you have to import the random module and call the function with a static random object.

Example:

```
import random
from random import randint
random.seed (40)
print ('Num1 -', random.randint(20, 45))

random.seed (20)
print ('Num2 -', random.randint (10, 30))
```

// Output

```
Num1 - 34
Num2 - 14
```

How Seed() Works

The *seed()* method is a random module that initializes a pseudorandom number generator. It saves the state of a random function to enable multiple execution of random numbers on the code on either the same machine or different machines.

The seed value indicates the previous random value generated by random generator. If no previous value, the current system time will be used. Call the seed first before calling the random number generator.

Example 2:

```
import random
random.seed (4)
print (random.randint (1, 200))
print (random.randint (1, 200))
print (random.randint (1,200))
print (random.randint (1,200))
```

/ Output

```
61
78
27
185
```

Uses of Random.seed()

1. It generates encryption key using the pseudorandom generator. An encryption key is an important tool in maintaining computer security. Seed() generates secret keys or codes used in protecting data from unauthorized access over the internet.

2. Random testing of numbers making it easy to optimize the codes. The codes output depends on the input data. The seed produces the same random number if you pass the same arguments to the seed () function.

3. It simplifies algorithm testing process.

Cryptographically Secure Random Generator in Python

Random numbers and any data generated using the random module is not secure. You can implement cryptography to securely generate pseudo-random numbers. The pseudo random number generator will have properties that will make data more secure.

A cryptographically secure random number generator returns a random byte. This random byte generated depends on OS random sources. A secure random number can be achieved through:

- Use of secret module to ensure secure generation of random data

- Using the os.urandom () function.

- Using the random.SystemRandom class

Example:

```
>>> import random
>>> import secrets
>>> num1= random.SystemRandom().random ()
>>> print ('A cryptographic secure number is', num1)
>>> print ('The secure bytes token is', secrets.token_bytes
(16))
```

// Output

```
A cryptographic secure number is 0.922173569673084
The secure bytes token is
b'\xd0R\xcd\xe5K\xacF\x13\xf3\x80\xae"9OQw'
```

Get and Set Random Generator State

A random module uses *getstate()* and *setstate ()* functions to determine the current internal state of a random number generator. This information is essential in generating a sequence of data or generating the same random numbers.

Random.getstate()

The *getstate* function records the current internal state of a random number generator. The recorded state is then passed to the *setstate* function to restore the state to the current state. If you change the state to its previous one, you will get the same random data.

Random.setstate ()

This function restores the internal state to its previous state. It restores random generator to state object that is, same state again. To obtain the state object, a call to *getstate()* function is made.

If you restore the previous state, it will enable you to reproduce or obtain the same random values again. If you use a different random function or pass different parameter lists, then this alters the state of the random generator.

Example:

```
import random
new_list= [2,5,7,8,10,12]
print ("Sample list", random.sample (new_list, k=4))
status= random.getstate() #storing the current state in status
object
print ("Another sample list", random.sample(new_list, 4))
random.setstate (status)
print ("Printing restored state", random.sample (new_list, 4))
random.setstate (status)
print ("Printing another restored state", random.sample
(new_list, 4))
```

// Output

```
Sample list [7, 8, 5, 10]
Another sample list [2, 10, 12, 8]
Printing restored state [2, 10, 12, 8]
Printing another restored state [2, 10, 12, 8]
```

Numpy.random (Using PRNGs for Arrays)

PRNG stands for Pseudo-random number generator. It uses the Python random module to help generate data or scalar random numbers. The *numpy.random* method enables you to generate an array of random numbers. The numpy package has multiple functions which generates n-dimensional array of random numbers.

The numpy package includes:

- *numpy.random.rand ()* which generates an n-dimensional array of floating point random numbers in the range of 0.0 and 1.0.

- *numpy.random.uniform* which generates an n-dimensional array of floating point numbers within a given range.

Example:

```
import numpy
array_list =[10, 20, 40, 30, 50, 20, 50]
```

123

```
random_choice = numpy.random.choice (array_list, k=1)
print ('selecting random choice for single array:',
random_choice)
multiple_array = numpy.random.choice (array_list, k=3,
replace=False)
print ('selecting multiple random choice array without
replacement:', multiple_array)

multiple_array = numpy.random.choice (array_list, k=3,
replace=True)
print ('selecting multiple random choice array with
replacement:', multiple_array)
```

// Output

```
selecting random choice for single array: [10]
selecting multiple random choices array without any replacement:
[20 20 10]
selecting multiple random choices array with a replacement:  [10
50 50]
```

Generating Random Numbers with Unique IDs

The UUID (Universally Unique Identifier) module in Python provides you with immutable UUID objects to enable you generate a unique ID. The UUID package consists of various functions generate universal IDs. It allows you to generate up to 128 bit long unique random ID and a cryptographic safe.

These unique IDs help in identifying users, documents, resources, or any information exchanged within a computing system.

To use the UUID object, you have to import the module in your development framework.

```
import uuid
getid= uuid.uuid4()
print ('Your secret id is', getid)
```

// Output

```
Your secret id is 3430e137-4f94-4528-9b64-222d77bd6cd9
```

Chapter Summary

Python consists of a list of libraries commonly known as modules for use with other programs. The math module allow you to perform various tasks. In this chapter, you learned how to:

- Import the math module into your program

- Refer functions in the module as module_name.function_name. The dot (.) operator means part of.

- Use the math module in the standard library

- Use python constants

- Use various math functions to perform various mathematical calculations. Some of these functions include: numbers and numeric representation, power and logarithmic functions, and trigonometric and angular conversion functions.

- Import the random module and import *randint()* from the random module

- Use Python random module to generate random numbers and how players can play dice game using both shuffle and choice methods.

- Use the seed algorithm to generate a pseudo random number. It uses the seeding value as the base when generating random numbers. The seeding method relies on the previous state of the random number and if no previous number recorded, it uses the current date system.

- Use and apply the *seed()* and *random.seed()* functions

- Cryptographically secure random generator in Python. This ensures you're able to secure your own data and information being exchanged from one machine to another.

- Use the *getstate()* and *setstate()* random generator functions to determine the current internal state of a random number.

- Use the numpy python package when working with arrays.

- Generate unique IDs using the UUID module.

In the next chapter you will learn about the date and time module.

CHAPTER FIVE:

Date and Time Functions

Introduction

Dates in Python programming do not have a data type on their own. To use the date's objects or the date function, you have to import the *datetime* module into your program.

```
>>> import datetime
>>> date = datetime.datetime.now()
>>> print (date)
```

// Output

```
2020-01-05 05:50:08.673261
```

The datetime method returns the year, month, day, and the system time during execution displayed in hours, minutes, seconds, and microsecond. The datetime module has various functions that return information on the date object.

In the above example, we defined datetime class inside the datetime module and then used the *now()* function to create an object with the current date and time.

Python keeps track of date and time in different ways. The datetime python module helps in tracking dates and time as well as converting the date formats. Time formats are expressed as floating point numbers in units of seconds.

The time module has multiple functions for working with the time format and conversion between representations.

Date and Time Manipulation

Date, time, and datetime in python are classes that provide multiple functions to handle date, time, time intervals, and date. Both date and datetime are Python objects, and once you manipulate them, you're actually manipulating the object itself, not its string or timestamp.

To manipulate date and time, you have to import the datetime module in your Python shell. The datetime class is classified into:

- Date class: This manipulates dates in terms of month, day, and year.

- Time class: It handles time formats in the form of hours, minutes, seconds, and microsecond. Time is independent of the day.

- Timedate class: It handles both date and time formats

- Timedelta class: It is used in the manipulation of dates and shows time duration.

- Tzinfo class: It handles time zones.

Using the Date Class

Before running datetime code, you have to import the module from the Python library, then make calls to specific date and time functions. The date class allows you to instantiate the date objects which represent the year, month, and day. For example,

```
>>> import datetime
```

The line above tells Python interpreter to import date class from the datetime module. Once you imported the date class, the next step is to create an instance of the date object.

To get the current date, you can run the following code:

```
>>>import datetime
>>>today_date=datetime.date.today()
>>>print (today_date)
```

// Output

```
2020-01-05
```

The *today()* method is part of date class functions and it allows you to use the date object to extract the current system date. You can also use *date.today()* method to return the current date.

You can also use the *date()* method, which acts as a constructor of the date class. In this case, the *date ()* constructor accepts three arguments: year, month, and day.

```
That is, today_date= datetime.date (2020, 01, 05).
```

You can also import the date class from the datetime object. This can be done through the following code:

```
from datetime import date
d= date (2020, 01, 05)
print (d)
```

Using Timestamp to Retrieve Date

A date object can also be created from a timestamp. A Unix timestamp is used to determine seconds in a particular date range. You can easily convert the timestamp format to date form using *fromtimestamp ()* method.

Example:

```
from datetime import date
d = date.fromtimestamp(1582145574)
print("Date ", d)
```

// Output

```
Date 2020-02-19
```

Using the Time Class

A time object can be instantiated from a time class. From the datetime object, import time class. To get the current time, assign the time class to *datetime.now ()* method.

Example: Using time class to get the current local time.

```
from datetime import time
tt=datetime.time (datetime.now())
print ('The current time is:', tt)
```

// Output

```
The current time is: 17:27:08, 384466
```

The tt variable is used to store the time value. When you call the *datetime.now()* method, it returns the current system time.

Example 2:

```
from datetime import time
t=time()
print (t)
t1= time(11, 34, 10)
print (t1)
```

// Output

```
00:00:00
```

```
11:34:10
```

Datetime Class

The datetime module has a datetime class with properties of both the date and time classes. The *datetime()* class accepts time and timezone arguments.

```
import datetime
date = datetime.datetime.now()
print (date)
```

Strftime () Method

The datetime object consists of formatting functions used to format the date objects into a string. The *strftime()* method is used to format a readable string and accepts a single parameter (format) to specify how the date string is returned

Example: Displaying the date based on the month

```
import datetime
d=datetime. datetime(2020, 1, 3)
print (d.strftime("%b"))
```

// Output

```
Jan
```

The *strftime()* method uses different control codes to produce different outputs. The different control codes represents different date formats like %y/%Y for years, %a/%A for weekdays, and %b/%B for months. If you use %Y, it will print the full year (i.e. 2021), but if you use a lowercase %y, it will print out (21) instead.

Example:

```
import datetime
d=datetime. datetime(2019)
print (d.strftime("%y"))
```

// Output

```
19
```

Example 2:

```
from datetime import time
now= datetime.now()
print (now.strftime('%A, %d %B, %Y'))
```

// Output

```
Sunday, 5 January, 2020
```

Some commonly used formats for the date class include:

Directive	Description	Example
%a	Weekday, short version	Wed
%A	Weekday, full version	Wednesday
%w	Weekday as a number 0-6, 0 is Sunday	3
%d	Day of month 01-31	31
%b	Month name, short version	Dec
%B	Month name, full version	December
%m	Month as a number 01-12	12
%y	Year, short version, without century	18
%Y	Year, full version	2018
%H	Hour 00-23	17
%I	Hour 00-12	05
%p	AM/PM	PM
%M	Minute 00-59	41
%S	Second 00-59	08
%f	Microsecond 000000-999999	548513
%z	UTC offset	+0100
%Z	Timezone	CST
%j	Day number of year 001-366	365
%U	Week number of year, Sunday as the first day of week, 00-53	52
%W	Week number of year, Monday as the first day of week, 00-53	52
%c	Local version of date and time	Mon Dec 31 17:41:00 2018
%x	Local version of date	12/31/18
%X	Local version of time	17:41:00
%%	A % character	%

Using Timedelta Methods

A timedelta object is used to determine any special day, date, or time. It can predict past and future periods. It doesn't print date or time, only calculates them.

To use the timedelta class, you have to import it from the datetime module.

```
>>> from datetime import timedelta
>>> print (timedelta(days=20, hours=4, minutes=45))
20 days, 4:45:00

>>> # display today's date
>>> print ('Today is on:' + str (datetime.now()))
Today is on: 2020-01-05 24:41:15.528684

>>> # retrieve future date: one year from now
>>> print ('A year from now will be:' + str (datetime.now()
```

```
+timedelta(days=365)
A year from now will be: 2021-01-05 24:42:20. 407012

>>> # calculate future date from current time
>>> print ('In one week and 2 days the date will be:'
+str(datetime.now() + timedelta(weeks=1, days=2) ))
In one week and 2 days the date will be: 2021-01-14
24:44:18.582465
```

You can make the *timedelta()* method more complex by adding arithmetic calculations to it. For example, use *timedelta()* to determine how many days passed after the New Year or calculate the number of days within a particular date range.

Example: Calculate how many days after the New Year

```
from datetime import timedelta
#obtain today's date
today=date.today()
new_year= date.year,1,1) #first day of the year
if new_year<today:
    print ('The new year has already passed with %d days'
%((today-new_year).days))
```

// Output

```
The new year has already passed with 5 days
```

Python Strptime() Method

The *strptime ()* method is a string for changing the datetime format. The method creates the datetime object from any date and time string.

from datetime import datetime

```
date-string = "3 August, 2019"
print("The date string is:", date-string)
dateobject = datetime.strptime(date-string, "%d %B, %Y")
print("The date object is:", dateobject)
```

// Output

```
The date string is: 3 August, 2019
The date object is: 2019-08-3 00:00:00
```

The above string represents date and time format and the format code equivalent in the form of %d, %B, and %Y to represent day, month, and year in full names.

Working with Different Time Zones

If you're working on a program that needs to display different time zones, you have to call the pytZ module into your program. The pytZ module allows you to display the date or time based

131

on a particular time zone.

```
from datetime import datetime
import pytz
local = datetime.now()
print("Local:", local.strftime("%m/%d/%Y, %H:%M:%S"))

tz_NY = pytz.timezone('America/New_York')
datetime_NY = datetime.now(tz_NY)
print("NY:", datetime_NY.strftime("%m/%d/%Y, %H:%M:%S"))

tz_London = pytz.timezone('Europe/London')
datetime_London = datetime.now(tz_London)
print("London:", datetime_London.strftime("%m/%d/%Y, %H:%M:%S"))
```

// Output

```
Local time: 2020-1-5 15:20:44.260462
America/New_York time: 2020-1-5 15:20:44.260462
Europe/London time: 2020-1-5 15:20:44.260462
```

The datetime objects created include the datetime_NY object and datetime_london object. These objects obtain the date and time of the respective areas based on the time zone.

Python Time Module

The Python time module provides functions used for manipulating time and converting time representations. You can use objects, numbers, and strings to represent the time class. To use these functions, you have to import the module in your program.

```
>>> import time
```

At the end of the chapter, you will be able to understand how to create time using epochs and time zones and represent time using floating points or tuples.

Python Time Using Floating Point Numbers

One way to manage time in Python is to use floating point numbers that indicate the number of seconds that have passed since the epoch era. That is, a specific starting point. The epoch is very essential when implementing time in Python project.

The Epoch Era

Epoch is used to manage time using floating point numbers. It represents an elapsed time since the starting of a particular era. An era is a fixed point in time which records a particular series of years.

The starting point identifies/ measure the passage of time of an epoch. For example, if epoch is defined on January 1, 1970 UTC at midnight (standard date format for Windows and Unix systems), then since epoch, the midnight date on January 2, 1970 UTC is represented as 86400 seconds.

This is simply so because a day has 24 hours, 60 minutes in an hour and 60 seconds in a minute. Therefore, January 2, 1970 is a single day after epoch:

```
>>>24*60*60
86400
```

Time can also be represented before epoch by indicating the number of seconds to be negative. Therefore, the epoch on midnight of December 31, 1969 UTC is -86400 seconds.

Though January 1, 1970 UTC is the standard epoch, there are other epochs used in computing. Different filesystems, operating systems and APIs use different epochs. For example, unix operating system use January 1, 1970 epoch while Win32 API use January 1, 1601 epoch.

To know your operating system epoch, use *time.gmtime()* method.

```
>>> import time
>>> time.gmtime (0)
time.struct_time(tm_year=1970, tm_mon=1, tm_mday=1, tm_hour=0, tm_min=0, tm_sec=0,
tm_wday=3, tm_yday=1, tm_isdst=0)
```

Python Time in Seconds

The *time.time()* Python function will show the number of seconds that have passed since an epoch.

```
>>> from time import time
>>> time()
1578308718.2490938
```

Time is measured in seconds in order to:

- Determine the difference between the two floating points in time.

- Use floats for data transfer. Floating point numbers are serializable and can easily be stored to enable data transfer from one end to the other. For example, if you want to have time represented in form of a string, pass the number of seconds from the *time()* function into the *time.ctime()* function.

Example: Time conversion in seconds into a string

```
>>> from time import time, ctime
>>> t_seconds=time()
>>> ctime(t_seconds)
'Mon Jan  6 14:15:50 2020'
```

The above code records the current time in seconds to the variable 't_seconds' and then passes the variable t_seconds as the argument to the *ctime ()* function.

The *ctime()* function returns a string inform of a timestamp which has the following attributes.

```
Current day of the week: Mon
The month: Jan
Day of the month: 6
Current time using 24-hour clock notation:  14:15:50 (hours,
minutes, seconds)
The year: 2020
```

The timestamp above is based on your current time zone. If you run the same code in a computer in different states, you will get a different timestamp. Therefore, the timestamp returned by the call to *ctime ()* is based on your geographical location.

The representation of time based on your physical location is known as local time and the concept of time representation is known as time zones.

Time Zones

A time zone allows us to conform to a standardized time within our region in the world. A time zone is defined using the Coordinated Universal Time (UTC) and takes into account Daylight Savings Time.

UTC and Time Zones

UTC is a standard for synchronizing or coordinating the world's time keeping. It acts as a transcendent standard that determines which time zone we are in. UTC is measured using astronomical time, which determines the Earth's rotation and its atomic clock.

Different time zones are determined by their offset from the UTC. For example, the North and South America use the Central Time zone (CT) which is usually behind the UTC time by either five or six hours. Therefore, the notation UTC -5:00 or UTC – 6:00 is used to represent the two states.

If you're in Australia or Sydney, the Eastern Time Zone (AET) is usually ahead of UTC zone with 10 or 11 hours. Therefore, the UTC notation is UTC + 10:00 or UTC + 11:00.

The reason behind why some parts of the world are either six hours behind or eleven hours ahead of the UTC is because they observe daylight saving time.

Daylight Savings Time

Summer months have longer days than nights while winter months have longer nights than days in some parts of the world. This is because some places observe Daylight Savings Time (DST) during the spring and summer periods to make better use of these long daylight hours.

In areas where DST is observed, the clock always jumps one hour ahead at the start of Spring. Then, during Fall, the clock will be reset to its standard time.

When representing time as a timestamp, you have to factor in the DST. The *ctime ()* function accounts for the DST.

Every function in the time module has the following attributes.

Sr.No.	Attribute with Description
1	**time.timezone** Attribute time.timezone is the offset in seconds of the local time zone (without DST) from UTC (>0 in the Americas; <=0 in most of Europe, Asia, Africa).
2	**time.tzname** Attribute time.tzname is a pair of locale-dependent strings, which are the names of the local time zone without and with DST, respectively.

Working with Python Time Using Data Structures

In the previous subtopics, we have used numbers, epochs, UTC, and strings to represent Python time. There are other ways you can incorporate the Python time module. This includes the use of primitive data structures like tuples to represent time.

Using Tuples to Represent Python Time

Tuple data structures are very important in the representation of time modules. Tuples allow you to easily represent time data. It abstracts some data items not needed to make it more readable. When you represent time using tuples, every tuple element will represent a specific element of the time.

Some of these elements include:

- Date: represents the format (year, month represented as an integer value from 1 to 12, the day of the month).

- Time: in the form of hours (24 hour format), minutes, and seconds

- Day of the week: this is an integer value to represent any day of the week where 0 corresponds to Monday and 6 represent Sunday.

- Day of the year

- Daylight savings time which is an integer value with

  o 1 to indicate daylight saving time

  o 0 to indicate the standard time

  o -1 unknown value

135

Let's look at an example on how to represent time module using tuples.

```
#time representation with tuple
>>> from time import time, ctime
>>> t_seconds=time ()
>>> t_seconds
1578321168.5871239
>>> ctime(t_seconds)
'Mon Jan  6 17:32:48 2020'
>>> time_tuple= (2020, 1, 6, 17, 32, 48, 50, 57, 0)
```

The t_seconds and time_tuple show the same time, but the tuple indicates a more readable interface to deal with components.

Using Python Time as an Object

When you use tuples, it just looks like a list of numbers, albeit more organized. The *struct_time* solves this tuple construct problem by calling the *NamedTuple* from Python collection library. This makes it easy to associate the tuple's sequence numbers using useful identifiers.

```
>>> from time import struct_time
>>> time_tuple= (2020, 1, 6, 17, 32, 48, 50, 57, 0)
>>> time_obj= struct_time (time_tuple)
>>> time_obj
time.struct_time(tm_year=2020, tm_mon=1, tm_mday=6, tm_hour=17,
tm_min=32, tm_sec=48, tm_wday=50, tm_yday=57, tm_isdst=0)
```

In Python programming, no *struct* data type is required since everything is represented as objects unlike other object oriented programs, where keyword *struct* and *object* are in opposition to each other. The *struct_time* is derived from the C programming language where the keyword *struct* is the data type.

When Python time module is implemented in C language, the struct type is called directly into the program by including the *time.h* header file.

Example:

```
#accessing elements of time_obj using the attributes names
>>> current_day_of_year= time_obj.tm_yday
>>> current_day_of_year
57
>>> current_day_of_month= time_obj.tm_mday
>>> current_day_of_month
6
```

Converting Python Time from Seconds to an Object

So far, we have seen the various ways you can work with time. In this section, you will learn how to convert different time data types. Converting different time data types depends on whether the current time is a local time or UTC.

Coordinated Universal Time (UTC) Conversion

Epochs rely on UTC for time presentation, not on time zone. Hence, seconds pass since epochs are not variables based on your geographical location.

When using a struct_time object, the time module may take the time zone into account or not. There are two ways to convert the floating point numbers representing time in seconds: UTC and local time.

To convert floating point seconds from Python time to UTC based struct_time, use *gmtime()*. The *gmtime()* function is a part of the Python time module. When you make a call to this function, it will return the system epoch as we have seen earlier in our epoch discussion.

```
>>> import time
>>> time.gmtime(0)
time.struct_time(tm_year=1970, tm_mon=1, tm_mday=1, tm_hour=0,
tm_min=0, tm_sec=0, tm_wday=3, tm_yday=1, tm_isdst=0)
```

The *gmtime()* function converts the elapsed seconds to a struct_time in UTC. The argument 0 used as number of seconds finds the epoch itself.

If you call the functions with no arguments then it will return the current time in UTC.

```
>>> import time
>>> time.gmtime()
time.struct_time(tm_year=2020, tm_mon=1, tm_mday=6, tm_hour=16,
tm_min=12, tm_sec=7, tm_wday=0, tm_yday=6, tm_isdst=0)
```

When using UTC in Python projects, you don't have to worry about DST, the time zone, or even location information.

Local Time

In most Python programs, you will use the local time rather than the UTC. There are various functions you can use to obtain local time from the number of seconds since the epoch era.

The *localtime()* works the same way as the *gmtime()* function and accepts options *secs* arguments to enable creation of struct_time using the local time zone.

```
>>> import time
>>> time.time()
1578328017.015449
>>> time.localtime(1578328017.015449)
time.struct_time(tm_year=2020, tm_mon=1, tm_mday=6, tm_hour=19,
tm_min=26, tm_sec=57, tm_wday=0, tm_yday=6, tm_isdst=0)
```

The '*tm_isdst=0*' since DST is very important when calculating local time object. The value can be set to either 0 or 1 based on whether the DST of a given time is applicable or not.

For example, in the US, Daylight Saving Time is applicable nine days later on March 10, instead of onMarch 1 where DST is not applicable. Therefore, to test whether the DST flag will change correctly, you have to add nine days into the number of seconds within a day (86400*9) to obtain the *secs* argument.

```
>>> new_localtime_sec = 1578328017.015449 + (86400*9)
>>> time.localtime (new_locatime_sec)
>>> time.struct_time(tm_year=2020, tm_mon=1, tm_mday=15,
tm_hour=19, tm_min=26, tm_sec=57, tm_wday=2, tm_yday=15,
tm_isdst=0)
```

When you run the code, you will notice that the *tm_mday* has jumped ahead to 15, the *tm_wday* and *tm_yday* have also changed due to sunlight saving time.

Other attributes used in determining time zone in *struct_time* include *tm_zone* and *tm_gmoff.*

Example:

```
>>> import time
>>> current_local_time= time.localtime()
>>> current_local_time.tm_zone
'E. Africa Standard Time'
```

The *localtime ()* returns the East Africa Standard Time Zone. The tm_zone determines the local time zone of your system.

Example 2:

```
>>> import time
>>> current_local_time= time.localtime()
>>> current_local_time.tm_gmtoff
10800
>>> current_local_time.tm_isdst
0
```

The current local time is 10800 seconds behind the GMT. Greenwich Mean Time (GMT) is a time zone without UTC offset (UTC± 00:00).

You can convert the 10800seconds to GMT by dividing with seconds per hour (3600). Thus the local time GMT +03:00 which corresponds to UTC +03:00.

If you ignore the secs argument when calling the *localtime()*, it will return the current local time in struct_time.

Converting Local Time Object to Seconds

To convert the local time object to seconds, *mktime()* is used. *Mktime()* accepts parameter t which is in the form of a normal tuple with nine elements or a struct_time object.

```
>>> import time
>>> time_tuple= (2020, 1, 6, 17, 32, 48, 50, 57, 0)
>>> time.mktime(time_tuple)
1578321168.0
>>> t_struct = time.struct_time(time_tuple)
>>> time.mktime(t_struct)
1578321168.0
```

Converting Time Object to a String

You can also use strings to manipulate the Python time instead of using tuples. String representation of time is its timestamp, which improves time readability and builds an intuitive user interface.

The commonly used functions for converting a struct_time object to a string include:

- asctime()

- strftime()

Asctime()

The *asctime ()* function converts a struct_time object and time tuple to a timestamp.

```
>>> import time
>>> time.asctime(time.gmtime())
'Mon Jan  6 18:44:19 2020'
>>> time.asctime(time.localtime())
'Mon Jan  6 21:45:01 2020'
```

The *gmtime()* and *localtime()* functions return struct_time instances for both UTC and local time. These instances are converted to a string timestamp using the *time.asctime()* function. *Time.asctime()* passes tuples as an argument instead of floating point numbers. The parameter passed to the function is optional. If no parameter is passed, then the current local time will be automatically used.

Strftime()

Strftime() works in the same manner as *asctime()*, but it has additional formatting options that allow you to format the string into a more meaningful manner. The string format time (strftime()) formats struct_time object or the time tuples to a more readable form.

Strftime() accepts two arguments:

- format: which indicates the order and form in which time elements in a string appear.

- t: which is an optional time format.

Format strings use directives (character sequences) to specify the time element. For example, %d specifies the day of the month, %m dictates the month, and %y represents the year.

Example: Output date using ISO 8601 local time standard

```
>>> import time
>>> time.strftime('%Y-%m-%d', time.localtime())
'2020-01-06'
```

Chapter Summary

In this chapter, you learned how to work with the date and time format. To manipulate date and time, a datetime module is needed to provide different classes and categories like date, time, datetime, timedelta, and tzinfo. You also learned how to:

- Use datetime objects by importing the objects before execution of a code

- Use the *date.today* function to print the current local time of the day. You also saw how to manipulate the function by indexing a particular day and print an individual date, month, or year

- Use the date.time object to obtain the current time in terms of hours, minutes, and seconds

- Use the *strftime()* function to format time as a string. You saw how to print time and month separately

- Use the timedelta object to estimate both future and past dates

- Calculate special days, such as the number of days left before your birthday based on the current time

- Use the *strptime()* string method to change the date format

- Work with pytz module to change the time zone

- Import the time module and manipulate time. You learned how to work with dates and times using epochs, time zone, and Daylight Savings Time

- Represent time using floating point numbers, tuples, and struct_time

- Convert different time presentations, suspend thread execution, and use *perf_counter()* to measure codes performance

In the next chapter you will learn about file processing techniques including how to open a file, read from it, write into the file, and close the files. You will also learn about file methods and how to use os and os. path modules.

CHAPTER SIX:

File Processing

What Is a File

A file consists of a contiguous set of bytes used to store a collection of related information in a disk. The data in the file can be anything and is organized in a specific format, such as a text file or an executable file. Files are stored in non-volatile memory, which stores data permanently. Non-volatile memory structures include hard disks, which are unlike Random Access Memory (RAM), which only holds data and instructions temporarily.

Components of a File

A file consists of three parts

1. File header: this is the metadata about file contents and it stores information about the file name, size, type, and properties.

2. Data: this represents the contents written in the file by the user.

3. End of file (EOF): this is a special character that shows the reader has reached the end of the file

All files are stored with a specific extension based on the type of the file. For example, an image has the extension .gif because it conforms to the specifications of the Graphics Interchange Format. There are different file extensions you can use when operating files.

File Paths

When accessing a file, you have to provide the file path, the specific location where the file is stored in the computer memory. This is possible because of the operating system stored in your computer as it prompts file handling by the user.

The file path represents a string that indicates the location of the file. The file path consists of:

1. Folder path: where the file is located in the file system. It can be in subsequent folders which can be accessed using the backslash \ in Windows or forward slash / in Unix.

2. File name: this is the unique name used in storing the file.

3. Extension: this indicates the file type. It is shown at the end of the file path followed by a period (.) then the file type. For example, myfile.doc

If you want to access myfile.doc stored in Documents folder and your current location is the User folder, you can access the file by providing the file path, for example:

```
users/faith/documents/myfile.doc
```

Once you open the file, you can either read from the file or write into the file.

Opening Files in Python

To use any file, you have to open it. This is done by making a call to the *open()* built-in function in Python. The *open()* function takes the file path as an argument to the functions. When the function is invoked, it returns a single file object that allows reading or modification of the file.

```
>>> sample_file = open ('test.txt') # opens a file in the
current folder
>>>sample_file = open (C:/Users/Faith/Documents/myfile.doc) #
using file path
```

When opening a file, you can specify the file mode, whether to read 'r', write 'w', or append 'a' content into the file. You can also open a file either in a text mode or binary mode. The text mode is the default form for opening files. The binary mode returns files inform of bytes and is mostly used when dealing with non-text files such as executable files or images.

File Operation Modes

Mode	Description
'r'	Open a file for reading. (default)
'w'	Open a file for writing. Creates a new file if it does not exist or truncates the file if it exists.
'x'	Open a file for exclusive creation. If the file already exists, the operation fails.
'a'	Open for appending at the end of the file without truncating it. Creates a new file if it does not exist.
't'	Open in text mode. (default)
'b'	Open in binary mode.
'+'	Open a file for updating (reading and writing)

Example:

```
sample_file = open ("sample.txt")
sample_file = open ("sample.txt", 'w')
sample_file = open ("kaa.bmp", 'r+b') #to read and write data in
```

```
a binary mode
```

When working with files in text mode, you have to specify the encoding type. Otherwise, your code may behave differently when using different platforms.

```
sample_file = open ("sample.txt", mode ='w', encoding = 'utf-8')
```

Buffered Binary Files

The buffered binary file type allows reading and writing into binary files written as open('sample.txt', 'rb') or open('sample.txt', 'wb').

When you call *open()*, the file object data returned is either a BufferedReader or a BufferedWriter.

Raw Files

A raw file type is used as the low-level building blocks for binary data and a text stream. The file is opened by *open ('sample.txt', 'rb', buffering=0)*.

Closing Files in Python

After carrying out all file operations, you have to close the file and free up the memory. Computer memory is a limited resource and once not in use, you should deallocate the memory by closing all opened files. To free up the memory resources, we use the *close()* method.

```
# file operations
sample_file = open ("sample.txt", mode ='w', encoding = 'utf-8')
sample_file.close()
```

If an exception occurs while performing a file operation, the program will terminate without closing the file. To prevent this from happening, you can implement Python Try and Finally calls to catch all exceptions in the program.

```
try:
    sample_file= open ('sample.txt')
finally:
    sample_file.close ()
```

With the try...finally method, you're assured of proper closing of the file even when an exception is raised. You can modify your program code using *with* statements. This ensures the file is closed once the block of statements leaves the *with* statement. A *with* statement is highly recommended as it provides a cleaner code and makes it easy to handle exceptions.

```
with open ('sample.txt', 'r') as my_file
        my_file.read("This code will automatically close your
file!")
```

Writing Files in Python

You can write new content or update python file with new data. To write to a file, you have to first open the file the call the write mode ('w'). You can also append 'a' data or exclusively create a file using the 'x' mode.

The 'w' mode can overwrite the previous content in the file if you're not careful. You can also use the *write()* method to write a string or sequence of bytes . The *write()* method can also return the number of characters written in a single file.

Example:

```
with open ('sample.txt', 'w' encoding –'utf-8) as fl:
        fl.write ('\nThis is a sample file')
        fl.write ('Python files')
```

If the sample.txt is not available, Python will create a new file named sample.txt. If the file exists, it is overwritten.

Reading Files in Python

For you to read a file, you have to open it in reading mode. You can use the 'r' mode to read a file character or use the *read ()* method to read a file. When using the *read()* method you can pass the number of characters you want to read as an argument *read (size)*. If the read size is not specified, the function will call to read up to the end of the file.

Example:

```
>>> fl = open ("sample.txt", 'r', encoding = 'utf-8')
>>> fl.read(4)  # reading the first 4 data elements
'This'
>>> fl.read(4)  # reading the next 4 characters including space
' is '
>>> fl.read()   # read up to the end of file
'a sample file \nThe file \nhas three lines\n'
>>> fl.read()   # reading past end-of-file returns an empty
string
''
```

As seen in the above program, the *read()* method returns a newline in the form of '\n'. If you reach the end-of-file and invoke the read method again, it returns an empty string.

You can also use for loop to read a file line by line.

```
>>>for line in fl:
>>>print (line, end= '')
This is a sample file
The file
Has three lines
```

The line keyword is equivalent to '\n' and prints data into a new line. Passing line as a parameter in the *print ()* function ensures you don't print two lines when printing data.

Alternatively, the *readline()* function can be used to read each file separately. The function reads the file up to the newline. It also includes the newline character.

```
>>> f1.readline()
'This is a sample file\n'
>>> f1.readline()
The file\n
>>> f1.readline()
'has three lines\n'
>>> f1.readline()
' '
```

Appending to a File

You can append to a file or write at the end of an existing file using the 'a' as the argument mode.

```
sample_file = open('sample.txt', 'a')
sample_file.write("Add this data to a new line")
sample_file.close()
```

The append functions updates an existing file with new data without overwriting it.

Python File Methods

Python has various methods used in file manipulation. Some of the commonly used methods include:

Method	Description
close()	Close an open file. It has no effect if the file is already closed.
detach()	Separate the underlying binary buffer from the TextIOBase and return it.
fileno()	Return an integer number (file descriptor) of the file.
flush()	Flush the write buffer of the file stream.
isatty()	Return True if the file stream is interactive.
read(n)	Read atmost n characters form the file. Reads till end of file if it is negative or None .
readable()	Returns True if the file stream can be read from.
readline(n =-1)	Read and return one line from the file. Reads in at most n bytes if specified.
readlines(n =-1)	Read and return a list of lines from the file. Reads in at most n bytes/characters if specified.

145

seek(offset , from = SEEK_SET)	Change the file position to offset bytes. in reference to from (start. current. end).
seekable()	Returns True if the file stream supports random access.
tell()	Returns the current file location.
truncate(size = None)	Resize the file stream to size bytes. If size is not specified. resize to current location.
writable()	Returns True if the file stream can be written to.
write(s)	Write string s to the file and return the number of characters written.
writelines(lines)	Write a list of lines to the file.

Python Input/Output Operations

A Python module offers various built-in functions to enable us to manipulate files in the Python prompt. The *input()* and *print()* functions are the standard input and output operations widely used. The io Python module provides facilities necessary to handle I/O operations. The I/O operations are categorized into three:

1.   Text I/O

2.   Binary I/O

3.   Raw I/O

Each of the categories has a concrete object or stream. Each of the stream object can either be a read-only, write-only, or support read-write options. The stream object enable arbitrary random access both forward and backward in any location or allow sequential access especially when using sockets or pipes.

The i/o streams are dependent on the type of data passed as arguments. For example, if a *str* object is passed to the *write()* method, the binary stream will generate a *TypeError.*

Text I/O

Text I/O streams receives and sends *str* objects. That is, if the secondary memory or backing store is made of bytes, then there is transparency in the encoding and decoding of the data. A text stream is created using the *open()* method. You can also specify the encoding, although its optional.

```
my_file= open ('file.txt', 'r', encoding= 'utf-8')
```

Binary I/O

A binary stream accepts bytes-like objects and generates byte objects. It doesn't require any encoding or decoding. The binary stream is applied on non-text data and in manual controls of text data.

A binary stream is represented with *open()*, which accepts mode string 'b'.

```
my_file= open ('file.txt', 'rb')
```

Binary streams are also available as byteslO objects in the system memory.

```
my_file=io.bytes(b 'this is binary data: \x00\)
```

Raw I/O/ Unbuffered I/O

This acts as a low-level building block of both binary numbers and texts streams. The raw stream is rarely used and it's created by opening a file in binary mode and disable buffering.

```
My_file= open ('file.txt', 'rb', buffering= 0)
```

The io module has specific built-in functions for handling data. The *input()* and *print()* functions are the standard input output operations widely used.

FileIO has OS level files with bytes of data and implements both the RawIOBase and IOBase interfaces.

Python Output Using Print()

The *print()* function is used to display output data on a standard output device or file.

```
>>>print('This is our first output to the screen')
This is our first output to the screen

num= 15
>>>print('The num value is:', num)
The num value is: 15
```

The actual syntax of the *print()* function is print(*object, sep= ", end=;\n', file=sys.stout, flush=false).

The object is the value to be printed, and the sep is a separator with an empty space character. The end ensures all characters are printed. The file is the object where all data values are printed with the default value being sys.stdout.

```
>>> print (2, 3, 5, 6, 7)
2, 3, 5, 6, 7
>>> print (2, 3, 5, 6, 7, sep='*')
2*3*5*6*7
>>>print (2, 3, 5, 6, 7,sep='#', end='&')
2#3#5#6#7
```

Output Formatting

If you want to make the output more attractive, you can use *str.format ()* method on any string.

```
>>> a=10; b=15
>>> print ('printing value of a is {} and b{}'.format (a, b))
```

Printing value of a is 10 and b is 15

The curly braces are placeholders. You can specify how the output is printed by using numbers or tuple index.

```
>>> print ('Welcome to {0}{1}'.format ('Python', 'programming'))
Welcome to Python programming
>>> print ('Welcome to {1} in {0}'.format ('Python',
'programming'))
Welcome to programming in Python
```

The str or bytes-like object can also be used in a file to both read and write to the file. String files opened in text mode can use StringIO in-memory stream. BytesIO is used to open files in binary mode.

Python Input

Input operation allows us to take input data from the user. To do this, an *input()* function is used followed by the string you want to display on the screen. The syntax is input([user data]) where user data is the input string you want displayed on your screen. The user data can be optional.

Example:

```
>>> name= input ("Enter your name:")
Enter your name: Faith
>>> name
Faith
```

In the above example, you have entered your name as a string.

Class Hierarchy

I/O streams are organized as a hierarchy of class during the implementation process. The streams have an abstract base class (ABC), which specifies the various categories of the stream, and a concrete stream class, which provides standard stream implementation.

The abstract base class supports the implementation of the concrete stream class by providing various implementation methods. For example, *bufferedIOBase* supports unoptimized implementation of *readinto()* and *readline()* methods.

At the top of I/O hierarchy is the IOBase base class ,which defines the basic interface to the stream. The class doesn't separate operation for reading and writing to a stream. Implementation of abstract base class methods are allowed to raise unsupported operation.

RawIOBase ABC extends the functionality of IOBase. It handles reading and writing bytes into the I/O stream. Subclasses of file I/O rely on RawIOBase to provide a file interface in the machine file system.

BufferedIOBase is an abstract base class which handles buffering on a raw byte stream. The BufferedReader and BufferedWriter subclasses are used to buffer readable, writeable, and both read/write streams. Random access streams uses BufferedRandom as an interface buffer.

TextIOBase ABC is a subclass of IOBase and it handles text streams and both encoding and decoding of text streams.

Importing Python OS Module

When writing complex programs in Python, it is essential to break the program into several modules. A module is simply a file with various definitions and statements. For example, a python file has filename followed by file extension. All Python files end with the extension .py. A python definition inside a particular module can be imported into another python module. You can also import the module into an interactive Python interpreter.

You can import modules into python interface by using the keyword import. For example, to import the math module, we use *import math*.

```
>>> import math
>>> from math import pi
 3.141592653589793
```

When you import the math module, all the definitions inside the module are available for our disposal. This allows you to import specific attributes and functions using the *'from'* keyword.

When importing modules, python locates the module definition from different places defined in the *sys.path* which contains a list of directories.

The OS Module in Python allows you to perform various operating system functions. It provides you with functions for creating a new directory (folder), deleting a directory, renaming the directory, or accessing the contents of the directory.

These OS functions allows you to interface with the underlying operating system running on your machine and perform various tasks.

Creating a Director with the OS Module

To create a new directory in Python, the *mkdir()* function from the os module is used.

```
>>> import os
>>>os.mkdir ("d:\\newdir")
```

This created a new directory in the path specified by the string in the argument of the function. Now open your drive D in Windows Explorer and locate 'newdir' folder created.

Switching Directories

You can switch from the current working directory to the new directory created and do all your operations there. This can be done through *chdir()* function.

```
>>> import os
>>> os.chdir("d:\\newdir")
```

This will change your directory path to the new directory created. To know whether the current working directory has changed, use *getcwd()*.

```
>>> os.getcwd ()
'd:\\newdir'
```

The *getcwd()* doesn't take any argument and it confirms directory path has changed by returning the new directory path. Any file operation carried will be saved in this new directory.

Note: Directory paths are always relative. If you set the current directory to drive D and then to newdir without indicating the preceding path, then the current working directory will change to d:\newdir.

You can change the current directory to its original path by passing ".." as argument in the *chdir ()* function.

```
>>> os.chdir ('d:\\newdir')
>>> os.getcwd()
'd:\\newdir'
>>> os.chdir('..')
>>> os.getcwd()
'd:\\'
```

Removing a Directory

To remove an existing directory, the *rmdir()* function is used. This function deletes the specified directory. For a directory to be removed, it must be empty. You cannot remove a current working directory. In this case, newdir cannot be removed since it's the current working directory. To delete it, you have to change it from working directory, then delete it.

```
>>>os.chdir('newdir')
>>>os.getcwd()
'd:\newdir'
>>>os.rmdir('d:\newdir')
PermissionError: [WinError 32] The process cannot access the file because it is being used by another process: 'd:\newdir'
>>>os.chdir('..')
>>>os.rmdir('newdir')
```

You can also list all the files and sub-directories within a particular directory using the *listdir ()* function. If no directory is specified, then the files and directories in the current working directory will be displayed.

The OS modules have a variety of functions you can use with the most common functions on how to work with directories. Other functions include:

1. *os.name*

This function is used to retrieve the name and other credentials of the operating system your Python program is running on.

```
>>> import os
>>> print (os.name)
```

2. *os.popen()*

This is a file object manipulation method that opens to a pipe or from a command. You can either read or write to the file based on the specified file mode.

```
import os
file=mku.doc
# popen() is the same as open() function
fl = open(file, 'w')
fl.write("Python Programming OS Functions")
fl.close()
fl = open(file, 'r')
text = fl.read()
print(text)
# popen() allows you to access the file directly through its
pipe
fl = os.popen(file, 'w')
fl.write("Your first lesson")
```

// Output

```
Your first Lesson
```

3. *os.close()*

All files opened with *os.popen()* are closed with *os.close()* or *close()*, just like the normal *open()* function. If you use *os.close()* on a file opened with *open()*, Python will throw TypeError.

Therefore we can use *os.close* or *close()* to close the above program.

```
os.close(fl)
```

4. *os.error*

This function raise an OSError in case of an invalid file or files that cannot be accessed by the operating system despite having the correct path, name, and argument type.

5. *os.rename()*

It is used to change the name of a file. The function only works if the file exists and you have the rights to change the file.

```
import os
file=mku.doc
os.rename(file, mkunew.doc)
```

OS Path Module in Python

This module has functions used to handle Python pathnames. There are different functions supported by the module like retrieving path names, merging files, and normalizing functions among others.

These functions take only strings and bytes as arguments. That is, you can only pass parameters of string objects or bytes to the OS path functions. The returned file name or path is of the same type.

Functions of OS Path Module

1. *os.path.basename (path)*: This function returns the file basename. That is, it returns the file name based on the path to its location.

```
>>>#using basename ()
>>>import os
>>>output= os.path.basename ('/users/dir.py)
>>>print (output)
'dir.py'
```

2. *os.path.dirname(path):* This function returns the directory name from the specified path. It doesn't indicate the path name, only the name of the directory is returned.

```
>>>output= os.path.basename ('/users/dir.py)
>>>print (output)
'/users'
```

3. *os.path.isdir(path):* This tests whether a particular path is an existing directory or not.

```
>>> output= os.path.isdir ("c:\\windows")
>>> print (output)
yes
```

4. *os.path.isabs(path):* A function to confirm whether the specified path is absolute or not. An absolute path is one that begins with a backslash in Windows and a forward slash in Unix system.

```
>>>output= os.path.basename ('/users/dir.py)
```

5. *os.path.normalcase (path):* In windows, this function converts the filename path into lower case and the forward slash is converted to backward slash. The path remains the same for Unix and Mac OS systems.

Both os and os.path modules provides you with a portable way of interacting with platform-dependent functions and perform various input and output file operations.

Chapter Summary

File input and output processes are very important in the operation of I/O streams. In this chapter, you learned:

- What makes up a file, why files are important in Python programming and file paths.

- To understand the basics in reading and writing into the file, learn how to open and close files as well as appending to a file.

- Different file processing modes and how to apply them in the manipulation of files.

- Various file functions and how to apply them in various file input/output operations.

- The import python os module and interact with various operating system dependent functionalities.

- How to use python input to prompt you to enter data into the system.

- How to use the *print()* function to display your output and format the output based on your needs.

- How to use os.path module to confirm the existence of a directory, create a new directory , and change the directory path to make it the current working directory.

In the next chapter you will learn exception handling, how to use else clause and finally clause, using exceptions for flow control and exception hierarchy.

CHAPTER SEVEN:

Exception Handling

Exception

An exception is any error that occurs during program execution. When an error occurs, a python program generates an exception to handle the error and prevent the exit of the program. Python has a variety of built-in exceptions that generate an error when something goes wrong in your program.

When an exception occurs, it forces the current process to stop and transfer the control to the calling process until the error is handled. If the error is not handled, the program will crash. Therefore, exceptions handle errors and any other special conditions within the program.

For example, function A calls function B while B calls function C . If an exception occurs during execution of function C, function C passes the exception to function B which is then passed to function A. Function C doesn't handle the exception but passes it to other functions. If the error is not handled at function A, an error message will be generated and the program will terminate.

If you suspect a certain code will generate an error, it's necessary to create an exception to handle the error.

Common Exception Errors in Python

- IOError: This error occurs when you cannot open a certain file.

- ImportError: An error is generated if Python cannot import or find the invoked module.

- ValueError: It occurs when the argument passed to a built-in function or operation has the right data type but an inappropriate value.

- KeyboardInterrupt: This occurs when you press the keyboard interrupt key (Ctrl + C or the Delete key)

- EOFError: This error happens when *input()* and *raw_input()* reach the end-of-file (EOF) without reading any data.

Catching Exceptions in Python

Exceptions are handled using a try statement. If you have a critical condition or operation that might result in exceptions, you can place the program code inside the try clause and the code that handles the exception in the except clause. The operation carried out after the exception is based on the program needs.

Syntax:

```
try:
    # statements for block operations
except:
    #if execution occur, execute this block of statements
else:
    #no exception, execute this block of statement
```

The else block is executed if no exception is raised in the try block.

Example: Python code to open a file and write into it without any exception

```
fl=open("samplefile.doc", "w")
fl.write("A sample file for exception handling!!")
exceptIOError:
print ('Error:No file available to read data')
else:
print ('You have successfully written content in the file')
fl.close()
```

//Output

```
You have successfully written content in the file
```

Example 2: Opening a file where you don't have access permission

```
fl=open("samplefile.doc", "r")
fl.write("A sample file for exception handling!!")
exceptIOError:
print ('Error: No file available to read data')
else:
print ('You have successfully written content in the file')
fl.close()
```

155

// Output

```
'Error: No file available to read data
```

The try-except statements catch all exceptions that occur in the program. This may not be a good programming practice since the method only catches all errors but the programmer doesn't know the root cause of the problem.

Argument of an Exception

Exceptions receive arguments which provides additional information the exception. This can be done by passing a variable in the except clause.

```
try
    Statements
except (exceptiontype, argument):
    Statements based on the value of argument
else:
    no exception statement
```

If you're writing code to handle a single exception, you can pass a variable to the except statement. If you have multiple exceptions, the variable is passed to the tuple of the exception.

The variable received either a single value or multiple values inform of tuple. The tuple will have error number, error string and error location.

Example:

```
#function definition
def temp_convert ( var):
try:
    returnint (var)
except (valueError, argument):
print ('\nThe argument passed is not a number', argument)
Temp_convert('xyz')
```

Except Clause with Multiple Exceptions

Syntax

```
Try:
    Execute operation statements;
Except exception 1:
    #block statements to handle exception
Except exception 2:
    #block statement to handle exception
Else:
# no exception found, execute this code
```

A single try statement may have more than one except statements. This is of great importance

156

if the try block has several statements that throw different types of exceptions. You can also create a generic except clause that allows you to handle different exceptions.

The block of code within the try clause is executed statement by statement. If an exception occurs, the except block is executed and the remaining try code is skipped.

Errors are always caught in the try clause while the except clause is invoked to handle the error. That is, if an error is encountered in try block, the execution of the try block is stopped and the control transferred to the except block to handle the error.

Else Clause

Python program allows the use of else statements. These statements are used to instruct a program to execute a specific block of code if no exceptions are found.

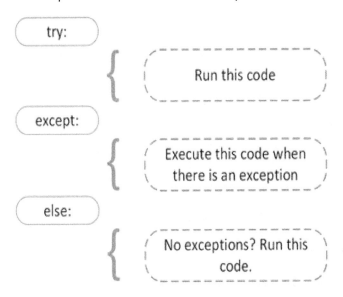

```
try:
        codecs.lookup()
except LookupError as error:
        print (error)
else:
        print ('No error found: executing the else clause.')
```

Since there is no exception when the code is run, the else clause is executed.

You can also insert the try block inside the else clause and catch any other exceptions.

Raising Exception

You can raise an exception in a program by using 'raise exception statement'. This breaks out the current code block and return exception statements back until the exception is handled.

In Python, we create exceptions using the raise keyword followed by the name of the exception with:

```
Raise exception_name
```

When you raise an exception, it interrupts the normal flow control of the program. When this happens, the Python interpreter looks for the code in its run-time-stack that can handle the message. The search begins from the current program state up to the end of run-time-stack. The execution process follow the order in which functions are called.

```
A try:except block is used to handle the exception.
```

The raise statement creates an exception object and leaves the program execution process to look for the try statement with a matching except clause in its run-time-stack. The raise statement can either divert a program execution if matching except clause is found or exit the program because a matching except clause for handling exception wasn't found.

The exception object has a message string to provide meaningful error messages. It also makes it easy to add more attributes to the exception.

Example:

```
>>> raise KeyboardInterrupt
Traceback (most recent call last):

KeyboardInterrupt
>>> raise MemoryError("An error occurred when loading memory")
Traceback (most recent call last):
MemoryError: An error occurred when loading memory
>>> try:
    val = int(input("Enter a positive integer: "))
            if val <= 0:
        raise ValueError("That is not a positive number!")
    except ValueError as ve:
        print(ve)

Enter a positive integer: -6
That is not a positive number!
```

Try...finally

The try statement can also have a finally clause. The clause can be optional and whenever used, it executes the program and free up the external resources. If you're working with files on a remote data center connected via a network or with a graphical user interface, you have to free up the memory after execution.

You must clean up the resources once done no matter what. Closing of the file, disconnecting from the network is always done in the finally clauses to guarantee you a safe execution.

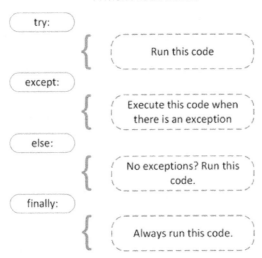

Example:

```
try:
    fd= open("sample.txt",encoding = 'utf-8')
    # performing a file operations
finally:
    fd.close()
```

Exception Handling for Flow Control

As we have discussed earlier, exceptions occur due to conditions that can't be handled by the normal flow of the program. In this case, exceptions are normally classified as errors. Although all errors are handled using exceptions in Python, not all exceptions are errors.

In normal flow-control of a Python program, instructions are executed one after the other using if statements, loops, and function calls. In these three constructs, the program flow-control is as follows:

In if statements, only one statement is executed at a time in a block of statements then the flow control is transferred to the first statement or line after the if statement.

In loops, when the end of the loop is reached, the program's flow-of-control loops back (is transferred) to the start of the loop to test whether the loop needs to be executed again. If no further execution is required inside the loop, then the flow of control is transferred to the first statement after the loop.

If you call functions in Python, the flow control is transferred to the first statement of the called function and executes the code. After function execution, the flow control is transferred to the next statement line in the program.

Therefore, the flow-of-control is a sequential process because when a call is made, it always executes the first statement in the program before proceeding to the next statement.

Example: Exceptions in flow control

```
def main()
  A()

def A():
  B()

def B():
  C()

def C():
  D()

def D()
  # processing
```

The above program is executing statements in function D previously called by function C. C is called by B, while B is called by function A, and A called by main (). If D gets an interruption on its current processing task, it has to send a message to main () to try something different. D can't send messages directly to main (), so it has to rely on the normal flow-of-control to send a special message to function C to 'try something different'. When C gets the message, it stops its current processing and passes the message to function B. The same procedure is followed until the 'try something different' message gets to the main() function.

Since program D couldn't communicate with main() directly or with function A and B, it creates an exception using the raise command.

When the exception message is created, it interrupts the normal flow-of-control of the program. Python evaluates its run-time-stack for a code to handle the exception message. When the code is found, a try:except block is thrown to catch the exception.

If function D had a try:except block on the code that raised an exception message, then the flow control would only have been passed to the local except block. This would have enabled D to solve its problems without transferring control to the main().

```
def main()
  A()

def A():
  B()

def B():
  C()

def C():
  D()

def D()
  try:
    # processing code
    if something_special_happened:
      raise MyException
  except MyException:
    # execute if the MyException message happened
```

Exception Class Hierarchy

A class hierarchy consists of a number of exceptions distributed across different base class types. In any programming application, errors occur when something unexpected happens. The errors can result from improper arithmetic calculations, a full or near-full memory space,

160

formatting errors, or invalid file references that raise an error.

The series of errors raised are considered as exceptions since they're non-fatal and allow the execution of the program to continue. It also enables you to throw an exception to explicitly catch or rescue the exception raised.

The exception hierarchy is determined by the inheritance structure of various exception classes. All raised exceptions are instances of a class derived from the baseException class. A try:except clause, using a particular class, can handle all exceptions derived from that class.

The hierarchy of the major built-in exceptions include:

```
BaseException
    Exception
     ArithmeticError
        FloatingPointError
        OverflowError
        ZeroDivisionError
     AssertionError
```

Most classes use keyword *exception* in the *baseException* and *Exception* in its parent classes. Subclasses uses the word *error*. A Python program inherits a series of *abcError* classes.

BaseException Class

The *BaseException* class is the base class of all built-in exceptions in Python program. A raised Python exception should be inherited from other classes. The BaseException class takes in a tuple of arguments passed during the creation of a new instance of the class. In most cases, a single string value is passed as an exception which indicates the specific error message.

The class also includes with_traceback(tb) method to explicitly pass the 'tb' argument to the traceback information.

Exception Class

This is one of the most inherited exception type classes. All the classes classified as errors are subclass to the *Exception* class. Therefore, if you create a custom exception class, it should inherit properties of the *Exception* class.

The *Exception* class has a variety of subclasses that handle the majority of errors in Python. Some of these subclasses include:

1. ArithmeticError: This acts as a base class for various arithmetic errors, such as when you're trying to divide a number by zero.

2. AssertionError: This is an error generated when a call to [assert] statement can't be completed or it fails.

161

3. BufferError: In Python, applications have access to a low level memory stream in the form of buffers. If the buffer memory fails, an error is generated: BufferError.

4. EOFError: This type of error is raised when an *input ()* reaches the end of a file without finding the specified file or any data.

5. ImportError: To perform advanced functions or work with complex programs in Python, you have to import modules. If the import statement fails, an importError will be raised.

6. LookupError: Just like in arithmeticError, a LookupError acts as the base class from which is inherited by other subclasses. If an improper call is made to the subclass then a LookupError is raised.

7. MemoryError: If a Python program runs out of memory or there is no enough memory stream to run the application, a MemoryError is raised.

8. NameError: This an error that occur when you try to call unknown name or use an identifier with an invalid name.

9. OSError: An error raised due to the failure of an operating systems

10. ValueError: It occurs if a method receives parameters of correct type, but the actual value passed is invalid due to some reasons.

KeyboardInterrupt

This occurs when the user presses Ctrl+C key combination. This creates an interrupt to the executing script.

GeneratorExit

The *generator* is a particular iterator which simplify iteration process with constantly changing values. It allows you to use the *yield* statement inside the generator code block. This type of exception allow Python to generate a new value when a call to *next()* function is made. When generator.close() method is invoked, a generatorExit instance is raised.

SystemExit

When you call *sys.exit()* method, a systemExit exception is raised. The *sys.exit()* function call closes the current executing script and then close python shell. Since this is an exception, you catch the exception before the scripts shuts down and exit by responding to the systemExit exception immediately.

Chapter Summary

From this chapter, you learned:

- That an exception happens when a certain condition interrupts the normal flow-of-control of a program.

- That if an exception is raised, Python first searches for a try:except block in the program's runtime stack to handle the exception. When the first statements in the try:except block handle the exception, then the flow control is transferred to the next line in the program.

- About common exception errors in Python and how to handle each of them.

- How to use the except clause and finally clause when handling exceptions

- About exception hierarchy

In the next chapter you will learn about graphics and image processing in Python as well as how to import a simple 2D drawing module.

CHAPTER EIGHT:

Graphics and Image Processing

Python Graphics

To make graphics programming more fun, Professor John Zelle designed a custom simple graphics library to make Python graphics as simple as possible for students. This library allows you to generate a graphical output using simple lines of codes.

You have to download the graphics.py library in your machine before you can use it. Save it in the same folder as the program you're creating.

Test your installation and import graphics:

```
>>> c:\> python
Python 3.6.3 (default, Jan 10 2020, 03:12:16) [MSC v.1500 64 bit (AMD64)] on win32
Type "help", "copyright", "credits" or "license" for more information.
>>> from graphics import *

|
```

If no error message generates, your installation was successful, and you can go ahead and start using the library.

Opening a Graphics Window

Open the code editor and enter the following code:

```
>>> from graphics import *
>>> win = GraphWin()
>>> win.getMouse()
```

The GraphWin is a call to the system to open a new window while getMouse instructs the system to active your mouse button. Save the command and run the code.

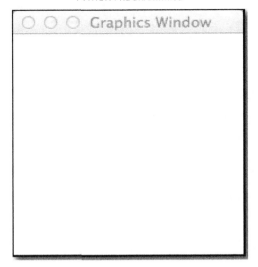

Drawing a Circle

```
>>> pt = Point(270, 140)
>>> cir = Circle(pt, 27)
>>> cir.draw(win)
```

To draw a circle, you have to call the circle, pass the parameter, and specify the point where the circle should be drawn. The *draw ()* function instructs the system to draw the circle in the graphics window.

You can refill the circle with any color of your choice by calling:

```
>>> cir.setfill ('red')
```

You can also build other shapes into your graphics by making the same changes.

Turtle Graphics

A turtle graphics is a robotic turtle made of different shapes that mimics simple moves. Turtle graphics is a great way of introducing graphics programming.

```
>>> import turtle
```

This allows you to import the module for handling turtle graphics.

Example: Assuming you have a turtle robot that initially has a starting point (0,0) in the x,y axis. You can pass a command that will move it 10 pixels.

```
>>>turtle.forward (10)
```

When you run this code, it will display the robot moving 10 pixels in the direction it currently faces, drawing a line as it moves. Give it another command to draw a circle.

```
>>> turtle.cirle(20)
```

This will change the robot image to a circle. The turtle library allows you to combine different commands to draw intricate shapes and pictures.

The turtle module allows you to use various commands, classes and methods interactively when running the module via the IDLE Python shell. The module provide primitive graphics in an object oriented and procedural language simply because it uses *tkinter* for all underlying graphics.

Classes of object-oriented interface

1. *TurtleScreen* class uses the graphics window as the playground to draw turtles. The *tkinter.canvas* and *scrolledcanvas* are arguments to the constructor class. *Screen()* returns an object of *turtleScreen* subclass.

2. *rawTurtle (Rawpen)* defines an object that draws on a *TurtleScreen*. A subclass Turtle is derived from RawTurtle.

Turtle Methods

There are various methods you can use to manipulate your graphics. They are classified into:

1. turtle motion (Move and draws methods, tell turtle's state, setting and measurement methods)

2. pen control (drawing control, color control, filing)

3. turtle state(visibility, appearance)

4. using events (onclick(), onrelease())

5. special turtle methods (clone(), get_poly())

Example: Moving the turtle to absolute position. If the pen face downwards, draw the line.

```
>>> import turtle
>>> tp = turtle.pos()
>>> tp
(0.00,0.00)
>>> turtle.setpos(60,30)
>>> turtle.pos()
(60.00,30.00)
>>> turtle.setpos((20,80))
>>> turtle.pos()
(20.00,80.00)
>>> turtle.setpos(tp)
>>> turtle.pos()
(0.00,0.00)
```

Example: Draw a circle centered at (0,0).

```
>>> import turtle
>>> turtle.home()
>>> turtle.position()
(0.00,0.00)
>>> turtle.heading()
0.0
>>> turtle.circle(40)
>>> turtle.position()
(-0.00,0.00)
>>> turtle.heading()
0.0
>>> turtle.circle(120, 180)  # draw a semicircle
>>> turtle.position()
(0.00,240.00)
>>> turtle.heading()
180.0
```

Image Processing

Today's world is data driven and different organizations rely on the use of images and video data to simplify processes. Almost 60% of graphics data in an application must be pre-processed. That is, the images must be analyzed, processed, and manipulated before being put to good use.

Python provides you with a plethora of algorithms on how to handle images. Image processing deals with various ways to handle image to image transformation. This involves both input and output image transformation mechanisms.

A computer vision is a field that deals with how computers understand or gain high-level information from a digital image or video.

An image processing algorithm accepts an image or a video as an input, processes the input, and outputs the results as an image or a video. A computer vision algorithm, on the other hand, processes the image or video inputs and constructively obtains meaningful information from processed data.

Working with Images in Python

An image is any 2-dimensional object with x and y spatial coordinates.

To use images in Python, you have to install the standard library package to handle images. PIL is one of the standard Python imaging library that provides Python interpreter with various image manipulation capabilities.

Other image processing libraries include:

1. *OpenCV:* this focuses on obtaining real-time computer vision with applications using 2D and 3D features, facial expression and recognition, robots, and human-computer interactions among others.

2. *Numpy and scipy library:* Used mostly in image manipulation and processing

3. *Scikit:* This library provides multiple algorithms used in image processing.

4. *Python Imaging Library (PIL):* Used when you're performing basic image operations like resizing, rotation of image, using different image formats or creating image thumbnails.

You can choose any Python library based on your image needs or what you want to do. In this chapter, we will focus on creating a basic image processing in Python.

Install Required Library

Install the required library to your machine

Once you install the pil library, you have to import the image module from pil.

```
from pil import image
#opening an image
img=image.open ('iphone.jpg')
#rotate image to 90 degrees and show
img=img.rotate(90).show
```

// Output

Convert and Save() Image

You can convert the image format from one form to another.

```
>>>img.save('iPhone.png)
```

This code will save a new iPhone image in png format on the same folder.

Resizing Image Thumbnails

```
>>> img.thumbnail (350,350)
>>> img.show()
```

Graphical User Interface (GUI)

A graphical user interface is an interface on the screen that allows interaction between the user and the system. The interface presents you with menus, text boxes, labels, buttons, menus, and main window that you can click with your mouse to perform a certain action. These GUI components are collectively known as widgets.

There is a wide range of widgets and a programmer can place them logically on the window making it easy for the user to interact with.

Event Loops

In any application, GUI waits for you to trigger an event or do something. For example, when you type something on the screen via an input box or click on a button with the mouse, it triggers an event.

At the back end, the GUI toolkit runs an infinite loop which is commonly known as an event loop. Events loops wait for events to happen, and then take action on the event depending on what the programmer wanted the application to do. If the developed application doesn't catch the event, then it's ignored.

When you're writing a graphical user interface application, always remember that you have to link up each of the designed widgets with the event handler to do something.

If you block event loops, the graphical user interface becomes unresponsive and it may appear to freeze (taking forever to load). If you launch an application in the GUI and it takes a long time to load, you should launch it as a separate thread or process. This prevents freezing of the GUI application, giving you a better experience.

Event Driven Programs

An event driven programming application is a program that relies on user inputs like clicking on a command button or choosing an item from a drop line list, using text box among others types of events. The program flow depends on the events happening by always listening for new incoming events.

When an event occurs, then an event handler decides what to execute and the specific order of execution.

Events programs are separated from the rest of the program code since an event driven program is an approach not a language. Event driven applications can be created in any programming language. These events leads to the improvement of the program responsiveness, throughput and flexibility.

Event Handlers

An event handler consists of functions or methods with the program statements that need to be executed once an event occurs. The event handler is a software routine for processing event actions like mouse movement, or keystrokes. Python event-driven programs rely on the event loop that listens to any new incoming event.

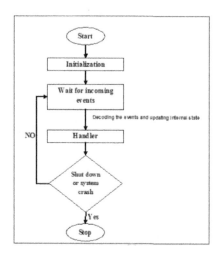

Binding and Events

The tkinter Python module relies on the event sequences to determine which event to bind to the handlers. The first argument passed to the event in the bind method determines the event to bind. An event sequence is represented as a string <modifier-type-detail> where the type field is used to specify the event. The modifier and detail provide further information to the 'type' but are not necessary required. Therefore, they are left out in most cases.

The 'type' determines which event to bind. For example, a mouse click event or an event as a result of key press has an input focus.

The tkinter application is always inside an event loop in which it enters the mainloop method. Tkinter is a powerful graphical user interface tool that allows you to easily handle events by binding python functions and methods to events in widgets.

$$widget.bind(event, handler)$$

If event A occurs and it matches the event description in the widget, then the associated handler is called with the old object that describes that event.

```
from tkinter import *

def single_button_click(event):
    '''
    Prints Single CLick
    '''
    print("Single Click")


def double_button_click(event):

    '''
    Prints Double Click then exits
    '''
    print("Double Click")
    import sys; sys.exit()

widget = Button(None, text='Mouse Clicks')
widget.pack()
widget.bind('<Button-1>', single_button_click)
widget.bind('<Double-1>', double_button_click)
widget.mainloop()
```

Example: Creating a motion event - moving a mouse inside the widget

```
from tkinter import *
def motion(event):
    print("Mouse position: (%s %s)" % (event.x, event.y))
    return

master = Tk()
msg = Message(master, text = 'Just Move it')
msg.config(bg='lightblue', font=('times', 24, 'italic'))
msg.bind('<Motion>', motion)
msg.pack()
mainloop()
```

Whenever you move the mouse inside the widget Message, the mouse position will be printed, if you leave the widget, *motion()* is not called.

TKinter provides you with diverse widgets like buttons, labels, textboxes, and other tools that you can use in a GUI application. The buttons display developed applications while canvas widgets are used to draw shapes like lines, polygons, circles and other shapes in your application.

The *mainloop()* function ensure the window continuously stays on the screen until you close it. If you don't include the function in your program, then the window appears and closes itself since you haven't indicated it should continuously run. Therefore, the *mainloop()* puts your code in an endless loop.

Python Predefined Events

```
<Button-1>
```

This event is used when you press the mouse button over the Widget. Button 1 is for the left mouse button, Button 2 is for middle mouse button while Button 3 is for the right-most mouse button. You can also use ButtonPress instead of just Button.

```
<B1-Motion>
```

This occurs when you move your mouse while holding the mouse button1 down. This provides the current position of the mouse pointer in the x, y members of the event object.

```
<Double-Button-1>
```

This is used when you double-click button1. You can also use triple-clicks, based on the prefixes, but if bound to both single click (button1) & double-click, then a binding call should be made to both.

```
<ButtonRelease-1>
```

If you release button1, the current pointer location is shown in the x & y members of the object event.

```
<Enter>
```

This is used when the mouse pointer is put inside the widget. (It shouldn't be confused with pressing the enter key)

```
<Return>
```

This is used when you press the Enter key

```
<shift-up>
```

This is used when you press the up arrow while holding down the shift key. You can also use a combination of Alt, Shift, and ctrl.

```
<Configure>
```

This is used when the widget changes size or its locations. You should provide the width and height of the new widget event object passed at callback.

Frames

Frames are used to organize your widgets in a window. They help you determine where to place them on a window though you can also use widgets without the frames. You can also insert multiple frames in a single window and insert widgets in them.

Example:

```
from tkinter import *

rootWindow = Tk()

rootWindow.geometry("300x300")
rootWindow.title("Hello World")

topFrame = Frame(rootWindow)
topFrame.pack(side=TOP)
bottomFrame = Frame(rootWindow)
bottomFrame.pack(side=BOTTOM)

rootWindow.mainloop()
```

When you run the code, it will create two frames, one at the top of the window and the other one at the bottom of the window. Frames create invisible rectangles on the window. Try out the code and see how python creates invisible frames for you to insert widgets.

The invisible rectangle is placed inside the rootWindow. If you pass an instance of rootWindow inside the frame class, a frame is created to fit the size of the rootWindow. Once the frame is created, *rootWindow.mainloop()* places the frame inside the window, where *pack()* can specify where it should be placed, whether at the top or bottom. You can also use the 'side' argument to place the fame anywhere you want inside the window.

Grid Layout

A grid layout is another way you can represent frames. It uses rows and columns to create frames. When using grid layout, you can think of the window as a spreadsheet with rows and columns to place your widget.

Example:

```
from tkinter import *

rootWindow = Tk()
rootWindow.geometry("450x100")
rootWindow.title("Hello World")

# topFrame = Frame(rootWindow)
# topFrame.pack(side=TOP, fill=BOTH)
# bottomFrame = Frame(rootWindow)
# bottomFrame.pack(side=BOTTOM)

label1 = Label(rootWindow, text="| Row-0, Column-0 |")
label2 = Label(rootWindow, text="| Row-0, Column-1 |")
label3 = Label(rootWindow, text="| Row-1, Column-0 |")
label4 = Label(rootWindow, text="| Row-1, Column-1| ")
label5 = Label(rootWindow, text="| Row-3, Column-0| ")
label6 = Label(rootWindow, text="| Row-3, Column-1| ")
label7 = Label(rootWindow, text="| Row-3, Column-2| ")


# label1.grid(row=0) This will also work because default column value is 0
label1.grid(row=0, column=0)
label2.grid(row=0, column=1)
label3.grid(row=1, column=0)
label4.grid(row=1, column=1)
rootWindow.grid_rowconfigure(2, minsize=20)
label5.grid(row=3, column=0)
label6.grid(row=3, column=1)
label7.grid(row=3, column=2)

rootWindow.mainloop()
```

// Output

Defining a label as shown above will allow you to enter text into your window as shown above. The created labels are placed in a grid layout by passing row and column number to the *grid()*.

Calling *rootWindow.grid_rowconfigure(2, minsize=20)* creates an empty row in the window. In the program, we have used row [0,1, and 3] and skipped row 2. If you don't call the *grid_rowconfigure()* function, it will put label 5 in row 2 even though you have specified o be placed in row 3 as shown below.

Therefore, *grid_rowconfigure()* and *grid_columnconfigure()* will help space rows and columns in your grid.

174

Python Asyncio Module

The Asyncio module provides an infrastructure for handling events in Python by writing a single-threaded concurrent code using subroutines.

Any event-driven program should have an event loop function.

Using an Event Loop

This is a function used to handle all the events in a particular code. It loops along the entire execution program and keep track of the incoming and execution of events. The module allow only a single event to loop in any given process.

```
Methods used
```

Loop=get_event_loop(): This is an event loop for the current program in the current context.

Loop.call_later (time_delay,callback,argument): The method makes an arrangement for a callback that is supposed to be made after the provided time_delay seconds.

Loop.call_soon (callback,argument): The method makes an arrangement for a call back immediately. The callback should take place after *call_soon()* is returned and the control is taken to the event loop.

Loop.time(): This method show the current time based on the events internal clock.

Asyncio.set_event_loop(): The current context to the loop is set based on event loop.

Asyncio.new_event_loop(): This creates and returns a new loop object.

Loop.run_forever(): This will run until a call to *stop()* is made.

Example:

```python
import asyncio

def hello_world(loop):
    print('Hello World')
    loop.stop()

loop = asyncio.get_event_loop()

loop.call_soon(hello_world, loop)

loop.run_forever()
loop.close()
```

// Output

```
Hello world
```

Chapter Summary

In this chapter, we are able to learn how to:

- Use the graphics library to create and manipulate images
- Use the turtle Python module to create graphical image

175

- Install the standard Python image library in a program

- Import an image from a particular library

- Work with images in Python and manipulate them

- Handle events and events-driven programming

- Use Tkinter in event-driven programming

- Work with the asyncio module

In the next chapter you will learn network and client server networking. At the end of the chapter, you will be able to explain how communication takes place between a client and server and how CGI applications communicate with each other.

CHAPTER NINE:

Network and Client/Server Programming

Python programming provides network access through two levels: lower level access and higher level access. You can access the basic socket support and its underlying operating system at the lower level. This enables you to implement a client server network for both connection-oriented and connectionless protocol.

The Python library provides high-level access to certain application level protocols like FTP, HTTP, TCP, and others.

Socket Programming

A socket provides a network connection and acts as the backbone for networking. Sockets transfer make information transfer between different programs and devices possible. For example, whenever you open your browser to search for information, you're creating a connection to the server for transfer of information.

Sockets can communicate within a process and exchange information between processes on the same device or between processes in different devices.

Sockets in Python

Sockets acts as interior endpoints designed for sending and receiving data. When connecting to a network, each network connection will have two sockets for connecting to the communication device and program. Each socket has an IP address and a port.

The socket, or node, on one of the connected devices listens to a specific port with the IP address while the other socket forms another connection. The server machine forms the listening socket while the client reaches out to the server with various requests. Each device has 'n' number of sockets determined by the port number used. Different ports use different protocols.

Some of these protocols and port numbers include:

Protocol	Port Number	Python Library	Function
HTTP	80	httplib, urllib,xmlrpclib	Web pages
FTP	20	ftplib, urllib	File transfers
NNTP	119	nntplib	Unsent news
SMTP	25	smtplib	Sending email
Telnet	23	telnetlib	Command lines
POP3	110	poplib	Fetching email
Gopher	70	gopherlib	Document transfer

The above port numbers and protocols form a socket module essential in network programming.

Socket Components

The socket library provides classes to handle a transport layer alongside an interface for connecting with other devices and programs.

Some of these components include:

Serial number	Term	Description
1	Domain	Domain protocol is used in transport mechanism and uses constant values like AF_INET and PF_UNIX among others
2	Type	It provides communication between two nodes. SOCK_STREAM is used for connection- oriented communication while SOCK_DGRAM is used for connectionless communication.
3	Protocol	This is a protocol identifier for domain and type socket components.

4	Hostname	This is a network interface which consists of: An integer represented as a binary number in the host byte order. A string that specifies the INADDR_BROADCAST address. A string which acts as the hostname or an IPV6 address in colon or dotted notation. A zero-length string to specify the address of INADDR__
5	Port	The server machine listens to a client machine making requests via one or more ports. In this case, the port may be a string that contains the port number, the service being requested or just a Fixnum port number.

Using a Socket Module

When creating sockets, you have to use the *socket.socket()* library function in the socket module. This can be done by:

```
S= socket.socket (socket_family, socket_type, protocol=0)
```

Where

The socket family: which is either in the form of AF_UNIX, AF_INET, or SOCK_DGRAM.

```
Socket type: uses SOCK_STREAM or SOCK DGRAM.
Protocol: By default it's always 0.
```

Therefore, you can import the socket library and pass two parameters to it as shown below:

```
Import socket
S= socket.socket (socket.AF_INET, socket.SOCK_STREAM)
```

The socket.socket is required by both the client and server machine to create sockets.

The socket.AF_INET parameter represent IPV4 address family whereas SOCK_STREAM is a connection-oriented TCP protocol.

Once the socket object is created, then you can use socket functions to create a client or server

179

program.

These functions include:

Server Socket Functions

Method	Description
S.bind ()	This function binds the specified address based on the parameter (the hostname and the device port number to the socket).
S.listen()	A method used for setting up and starting a TCP listener.
S accept	It passively allow connection through the TCP client and waits until connection is established (blocking)

Client Socket Functions

Method	Description
S connect()	Used to actively initiate a TCP server connection.

General Socket Functions

Method	Description
S recv()	To receive a TCP message
S.send()	For transmission of TCP message
S.recvfrom()	For receiving UDP messages
S.sendto()	Transmission of UDP messages
S.close()	Function to close the socket
Socket.gethostname()	Function to obtain the hostname of the

	device

Connection to the Server

A server is a powerful computing device or program used for managing network resources. A server can be connected on the same computer or locally connected to other computer devices or through a remote connection. There are different types of servers you can create, for example, a database server, printer server, and network server amongst others.

Example 1: Program to connect to server

```
import socket
s=socket.socket(socket.AF_INET, socket.SOCK_STREAM)
s.bind((socket.gethostname(),1234))#port number can be anything between 0-65535

s.listen(5)

while True:
    clt,adr=s.accept()
    print(f"Connection to {adr}established")
    #f string is literal string prefixed with f which
    #contains python expressions inside braces
    clt.send(bytes("Socket Programming in Python","utf-8 "))
    #to send info to clientsocket
```

From the above example, to create a socket, you have to first import the module. Then, use the socket.socket function to create a server socket.

The *listen ()* function allows connection to the server, with parameter 5 being the queue to multiple simultaneous connections. You can pass any parameter to the function with the minimum number being 0. If no parameter is specified, a default parameter zero is used.

The while loop accept all connections to the server. Clt and adr represent client object and address respectively. The print statement only prints the address and the port number of the connected device on the client socket. The *clt.send ()* function is used to send clients data in bytes.

Example 2: Connecting to Google website

```
#connecting to google website
import socket
import sys
try:
    s = socket.socket(socket.AF_INET, socket.SOCK_STREAM)
    print "successful creation of the socket"
except socket.error as err:
    print "socket creation failed: error message %s" %(err)

# default port for socket
port = 80

try:
    host_ip = socket.gethostbyname('www.google.com')
except socket.gaierror:  # throw exception to show it could not resolve the host

    print "there was an error incurred when resolving the host"
    sys.exit()

# connecting to the server
s.connect((host_ip, port))

print "Socket connection to Google is successful\
on port == %s" %(host_ip)
```

181

// Output

```
Successful creation of socket
Socket connection to Google is successful
On port ==173.194.40.19
```

Sometimes a socket error occurs when connecting to the server. In this case, a socket error is thrown, and for you to connect to the server, you have to use the IP address of the server.

To get the server IP address, you can type the following code in the command prompt:

```
$ping www.google.com
```

or use the Python program to obtain the IP address.

```
import socket
ip=socket.gethostbyname('www.google.com')
Print ip
```

Connection to Client Device

A client device is the computer that receives information or services from the server machine. In a client-server architecture, the client requests for services or resources from the server and the server provides the services to the client. For example, use your web browser like Google Chrome or Mozilla Firefox to request a particular webpage from the web server.

Example: Client-side requests

```
import socket
s=socket.socket(socket.AF_INET, socket.SOCK_STREAM)
s.connect((socket.gethostname(), 2346))
msg=s.recv(1024)
print(msg.decode("utf-8"))
```

This code imports a socket module and then creates the socket. *Connect()* creates a connection between the client and server machine by specifying the hostname and the port number.

The *recv()* method is used by the client to receive information from the server. The information is stored in a different variable message. The message is transferred in bytes.

Note: *gethoname()* method is used where the client and server are on the same machine.

Example: Python socket server connection using a local host IP address

```
import socket
serv = socket.socket(socket.AF_INET, socket.SOCK_STREAM)
serv.bind(('0.0.0.0', 8080))
serv.listen(8)
while True:
    conn, addr = serv.accept()
    from_client = ''
    while True:
        data = conn.recv(4096)
        if not data: break
        from_client += data
        print from_client
        conn.send("SERVER CONNECTION\n")
    conn.close()
    print 'Disconnection of client device'
```

This program binds the socket object to the local host using the port number 8080 which acts as the socket server. When the client device connects to the server using the specified address, the server will listen for the data requested and store it in the variable named 'data'.

The program then logs the client data using the 'print' output operator, which sends a message string to the client 'Server Connection'.

On the client side:

```
import socket
client = socket.socket(socket.AF_INET, socket.SOCK_STREAM)
client.connect(('0.0.0.0', 8080))
client.send("CLIENT device\n")
from_server = client.recv(4096)
client.close()
print from_server
```

The client socket connection code establishes a socket connection with the server. This only happens when the server program is currently running.

Execution of Client Server Programs

To execute client server program, open a command prompt and navigate to where you have created the client server program then type the following command:

```
py server.py
```

Server.py is the file name of the server. Once the server is running, you can execute a client program. This is done by typing the following command in a new command prompt window:

```
py client.py
```

where the client.py is the filename of the client program.

When the client device calls for *connect()* to establish a connection with the server, it initiates a three-way handshake. The three-way handshake is very important in socket communication as it ensures the network connection is reachable from both sides. That is, the client can reach the server and vice versa. The client and server exchange data using *send()* and *recv()* methods.

Communication Breakdown

The client and the server communicate with each other in the following ways:

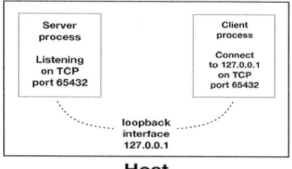

Host

If you're using the loopback interface 127.0.0.1 (IPV4 address or the IPV6 address::1), then the data will not go beyond the host or touch the external network. The interface is always within the host.

Application programs rely on the loopback interface to communicate with other programs that run on the host. This improves application security and isolation via the external network. Since the communication happens within the host, there is no threat from external sources.

This type of communication is applied in an application server with its own private database. The database is configured to be used by other servers or configured to listen for all connections on a loopback interface only. Any other hosts on the network can't connect to it.

If another IP address is used other than 127.0.0.1 on the network, it will be bound on an Ethernet interface connected to an external network. This allows you to connect to other hosts outside the localhost network.

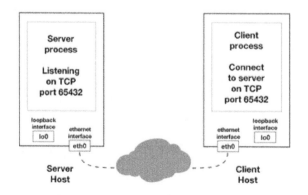

Multiple Communications

For the communication to go until the client receives all information, a while loop is used.

```
Import socket

S= socket.socket( socket. AF_INET, Socket.SOCK_STREAM)

S.connect((socket gethostname (), 2346))

While true;

Msg= s.recv(6)

Print (msg.decode("utf-8))
```

In the above program, the message will receive six bytes at each transfer. The program is not terminated at the end since the actual file size transferred between the client and server is unknown. To ensure the program terminates at the end, you can add the following code to the client side.

```
Complete_info="

while True:

msg=s.recv(6)

if len(msg)<=0:

break

complete-info +=msg.decode("utf-8")

print (complete-info)
```

On the server side, the *close()* method is used.

```
ctl.close()
```

The above block code check the size of the information and print it in a buffer of two bytes at a time. When the information transfer is completed, the connection is terminated.

Transferring Python Objects

Jut like other programming languages, Python socket programming enables you to transfer objects such as tuples, data sets, and dictionaries. Transfer of objects is achieved through the Python pickle method.

The pickle method is used during serialization or deserialization of objects in python.

Example:

```
Import pickle
Example=[1, 2, 'abc']
Msg=pickle.dumps (example)
Print (msg)
```

// Output

$$b'x80x03] qx00 (kx01x02x00x00x00abcqx01e'$$

The example variable in serialized using the *dump()* function. The output of this program starts with 'b' indicating the program is converted to bytes. You can also implement the pickle module when you want to transfer objects between clients and the server.

How to Transfer Objects

The pickle module can allow you to transfer anything via the network. The program below will enable you to transfer information from the server side to the client side device.

On the server side:

```
import socket
import pickle

x=8
s=socket.socket(socket.AF_INET, socket.SOCK_STREAM)
s.bind((socket.gethostname(), 2133))   #binding tuple
s.listen(7)
while True:
    clt , adr = s.accept()
    print(f"Connection to {adr}established")

    y={1:"Client", 2:"Server"}
    mymsg = pickle.dumps(y)   #the msg to be printed
    mymsg = {len(mymsg):{x}}"utf-8") + mymsg
    clt.send(mymsg)
```

In this server-side program, variable y acts as the python object that is sent from the server to the client machine. To send the message down to the client, the object is serialized using *dumps ()* and then converted to bytes.

Client-side program to receive data:

```
import socket
import pickle
x=8
s=socket.socket(socket.AF_INET, socket.SOCK_STREAM)
s.connect((socket.gethostname(), 2133))

while True:
    complete_info = b''
    rec_msg = True
    while True:
        mymsg = s.recv(8)
        if rec_msg:
            print(f"The length of message = {mymsg[:x]}")
            z = int (mymsg[:x ] )
            rec_msg = False
        complete_info += mymsg
        if len(complete_info)-x == z:
            print("Recieved complete information")
            print(complete_info[x:])
            y = pickle.loads(complete_info[x:])
            print(y)
            rec_msg = True
complete_info = b''
print(complete_info)
```

186

// Output

```
Sending objects using socket programming in Python
```

The first while loop will help you keep track of the information sent—whether it is complete or incomplete using complete_info—as well as know the length of the message received using rec_msg. As the message is being received, it is printed in a buffer of 8 bytes. You can choose any size you want to the buffer to be.

When the message is fully received, print received complete information then deserialize the message using the *loads()* method.

Why You Should Use Sockets to Send Data

All internet based applications operate in real-time, thus a great need to implement sockets programming in the networking code. Some of the apps that rely on socket programming include:

1. Chatting apps like WhatsApp, Slack, and WeChat.

2. Web pages with live notifications like Facebook, Twitter, eBay, etc.

3. IoT devices like Nest and August Locks.

4. Real-time data dashboards like use of Coinbase web page.

5. A multiplayer online game.

Python programming uses synchronous execution of programs; hence it was built to be more robust and support socket programming.

Sockets allow data to be streamed (sent and received) at any time.

Python provides a socket class that makes it easy for the programmers to implement a socket object.

CGI Programming

Python programming is used in the implementation of Common Gateway Interface (CGI) through the Hyper-Text Transfer Protocol (HTTP). It has a set of standards that defines how information is exchanged between a web user and an application program, that is, passing of information between a webserver and a custom script.

If a user requests for information from a certain web page, the web server sends back the requested information into the web page. The server device or program passes information into all application programs that process data before sending back an acknowledgement message. Passing information back and forth between the server and the application forms a common gateway interface.

The HTTP server invokes a CGI script to allow processing of user inputs submitted via the HTML <form> element. When a client makes a request, the server creates a script shell environment where it stores information about the request, the client's hostname, requested URL, the message query string, and any other information requested. The server then executes the script and sends the output results back to the client.

The input script is connected to the client and the server reads data from the input form this way or pass the data submitted via the form through a query string which acts as part of the URL.

The CGI programs are dynamically written and generate user inputs that respond to input data or a web page that interacts with the server software.

How Information Passing Works

1. When a user opens a web browser and click on a hyperlink to a particular webpage or its Uniform Resource Locator (URL),

2. The browser contacts the HTTP server and demand for the URL.

3. The web server parses the URL of the requested page and look for the specific filename of the requested information.

4. If the file is found, the request is sent back.

5. The web browser accepts the response back from the web server.

6. The response is either the received file or an error message to alert the user the file was not found.

When you request for a specific directory, the HTTP server executes the program and displays the output in your browser instead of sending back the file.

CGI Configuration

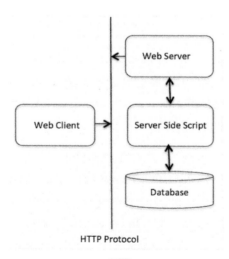

HTTP Protocol

The Python CGI architecture works in the following ways:

1. Requires you to specify the user running the web server

2. Analyzes the server configuration and find out if it is possible to run the scripts in a particular directory.

3. Analyzes file permission rights.

4. Makes sure the written scripts are clear, easily readable, and executable by the user of the web browser.

5. Ensures the Python script's first line represent the web server run by the interpreter.

Before you configure the cgi program, ensure the web server supports the cgi program and it is well configured. CGI programs executed in the HTTP server are all in a pre-configured device. The files are stored with an extension *.cgi*, but you can also store the files with the extension *.py*.

Python CGI Program Structure

The CGI scripts output has two parts: modules and functions. A black line separates each Python script.

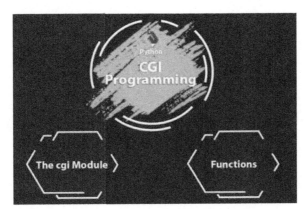

The CGI Module

The Python cgi module helps debug scripts and find solutions to various situations. The module can also help you to upload a file from a form. The script output results into two parts separated by a black line. The module consists of a number of headers to define what kind of data is following to the client. The header part instructs the clients to expect a certain type of data.

To use the module, you have to import it to your program.

```
>>>import cgi
```

Once you import the module, you can activate an exception handler to catch errors on the web browser. The exception will give a detailed report in the web browser in an event of error.

```
>>> import cgitb
>>>cgitb.enable()
```

If you want to store the report in the file, you have to add the filename to store the report and specify the file path.

```
>>> cgitb.enable (display=0, logdir='path to the directory')
```

CGI Header Section

```
print ("Content-Type : text/html")

print ("<html>")
print ("<head>")
print ("<title>My First CGI-Program </title>")
print ("<head>")
print ("<body>")
print ("<h3>This is HTML's Body section </h3>")
print ("</body>")
print ("</html>")
```

You can save the header section as header.py and run the code. The output of this program will be:

```
This is HTML's Body section
```

The Content-Type: text/html printed on the first line specifies the type of content to be displayed by the browser. The above program is a basic CGI program using the HTML tags. The written scripts can interact with external systems like RDBMS to exchange information.

All HTTP header section should be in the form of:

```
HTTP field Name: Field content
```

Example: HTML form with Python cgi-bin folder

```
<!doctype html>
<html>
<head>
<title>Example of python web file</title>
</head>
<body>
<form name="pytform" method="POST" action="/cgi-bin/form.py">
  <input type="text" name="firstname" />
  <input type="submit" name="submit" value="Submit" />
</form>
</body>
</html>
```

This script points to the following cgi program.

```
#!/usr/local/bin/python3.6
print("Content-Type: text/html")
print()

import cgi,cgitb
cgitb.enable() #for debugging
form = cgi.FieldStorage()
name = form.getvalue('firstname')
print("Name of the user is:",name)
```

The #!/usr/local/bin/python3.6 indicates the location of Python installation. Then, import the cgi and cgitb modules to handle any exception. *Cgitb.enable()* helps report errors.

The form variable is used to store the cgi class FieldStorage, thus, making the form function as a data dictionary. The *getvalue()* function extracts the name supplied by the user in the input HTML form. Use the *print()* to display the name of the user.

Components of HTTP Header

This table consists of common HTTP headers frequently used in CGI programming.

Value	HTTP Header	Description
Text/tml	Content type	This is a MIME string used to define the file return type format.
Date	Expires	This shows the expiry date/time. It indicates specific date when information will be invalid. A browser uses this header information to determine when to refresh a browser. A valid date string is in the form of 01 Jan 2020 08:00:00 GMT
URL	Location	This returns the url of the requested file. The url redirects to any file requests.
String	Set-Cookie	A unique field that sets passed cookies through the string.
N	Content-length	This header returns the file or data length inform of bytes. This format uses the length value to determine the estimated download time of the file.
Date	Last-modified	It defines the last date the resources were modified.

CGI Environment Variables

CGI programs have access to the environment variable listed below. These variables are very important when writing a CGI program.

Environment Variables	Description
CONTENT_TYPE	describes the data-type of the content
HTTP_COOKIE	returns the visitor's cookie if one is set
CONTENT_LENGTH	It is available for POST request to define the length of query information
HTTP_USER_AGENT	defines the browser type of the visitor
PATH_INFO	defines the path of a CGI script
REMOTE_HOST	defines the host-name of the visitor
REMOTE_ADDR	defines the IP Address of the visitor
REQUEST_METHOD	used to make request & the most common methods are - GET and POST

Example:

```python
#!/usr/bin/python

import os

print "Content-type: text/html;
print "<font size=+5> CGI Environment Variable</font><\br>";
for param in os.environ.keys():
    print "<b>%20s</b>: %s<\br>" % (param, os.environ[param])
```

Chapter Summary

In this chapter, you learned about networks and client/server programming using sockets. A Python program is able to provide a network access through both low- and high-level network access. You also learned how:

- The lower level access provides you with basic support to socket programming as well as allow you to implement both client and server network connections.

- The high level access is implemented through the HTTP,FTP, and TCP protocols.

- A socket in one of the connected devices listens to a specific port with the IP address while the other socket forms another connection. Sockets in python programming are designed for sending and receiving data between various devices with each socket having an IP address and a port number.

- The various port numbers and protocols form a socket module.

- The different classes for handling transport layer and provide an interface to connect to other devices.

- To import the socket module and how to connect to the server

- You can connect to google website

- Connect to a client device

- Communication takes place between the client server architecture.

- The importance of using sockets in sending data between devices in real-time.

- Basics of CGI programming

FINAL WORDS

Python programming is an Object Oriented programming language that allows you to design, develop, and implement robust programs. The programs use algorithms and information processing tools to develop applications. Developing any program to solve a certain problem requires that you first define the problem. Once you're able to define the program, you can come up with the program needs in terms of inputs and processes, which need to be followed in order to come up with the solution to the problem.

Major programming languages use algorithms when coming up with solutions to solve problems. An algorithm is a set of instructions that must be followed in order to perform a particular task or solve certain problem. In computer programming, algorithms act as recipes that describe the procedures necessary to achieve a set goal. You need to provide the input data taken by your computer system for processing. Following these predetermined procedures will result in a particular output. Algorithms in Python programming are intended to instruct Python interpreters what needs to be done, and they do exactly that.

Programs designed in Python can be represented in the form of flow charts or use of English-like statements known as pseudocode. Flow charts represent data in the form of inputs, processes, and outputs. Inputs involve the use of computer hardware and software to enter data into the computer.

Computer software is the term for programs designed to perform various tasks. These programs are classified into applications software, system software, and programming languages. In this chapter, we have focused on the use of programming languages, in particular, the Python programming language, to develop and implement programs.

We learned how to use the Python interactive shell and how to execute a simple python script. In our second chapter, we learned how to use Python strings. Strings are a built-in data type.

We have learned how to create a string of variables and how to access a single character from that string. Another important feature you learned is string slicing, which allows you to return sub-parts of a string in a certain sequence using built-in methods to manipulate strings.

Data sequences is another built-in data type that consists of a series of values held together by a container. A sequence ensures various objects and values are organized in an efficient manner. It consists of strings, lists, tuples, xrange objects, use of buffers, and byte arrays. As discussed in the previous chapter, strings consists of an array of elements whereas a list is a group of elements organized in a specific order.

Lists are essential in the implementation of sequence protocol. It enables you to easily add and remove elements from a sequence. Tuples work similar to lists except that they're immutable. You can't add, delete, or change elements created using tuples. Tuples prevents you from making any accidental changes to your program as well as allow for fast execution of lists.

You also learned how to use string concatenation, check for string membership sequence, and slicing. You learned various sequence methods used in manipulating data like *len()*, *count()*, and *index()*. You are also now able to create sets and manipulate them using set functions.

The Python dictionary allows you to add, change, or remove elements from a dictionary. Dictionary use a key and a value to make calls to a function. Elements in a dictionary are organized to retrieve data elements using a key. Learn how to add elements to the dictionary and also remove elements from a dictionary.

In Chapter Four, we learned how to use the math module to perform mathematical calculations. The math module defines two common constants used in calculations: *pi* and *Euler's number*. Python properties are accessed via *math.pi* while the functions. Other constants used in Python include *inf* and *nan*.

Python math functions support different classes in its standard library. These classes include: numbers and numeric representations, power and logic functions, and trigonometric and angular conversion functions. Each of these classes have functions which can perform a specific tasks.

Python random module uses pseudo-random number generator tool to generate random numbers for use. The generated numbers are in the range of 0.0 to 1.0. Some of the functions used in generating random numbers include *randint()*, *randrange()*, *sample()*, *shuffle ()*, and *choice()*. In this chapter, we discussed how to apply each of the random functions to generate random integer numbers. We also discussed how you can apply *randint ()* to determine a lucky draw in a game.

A Python *seed ()* function is used to get random numbers. Then, the seed number is passed to a pseudorandom algorithm that generates random sequence bytes. The pseudorandom generator rely on previously generated values. The *seed()* initiates the pseudorandom number generator. It uses the seeding value as the base when generating random numbers. If the seeding value is unavailable, then it automatically uses the current date.

The seed value always indicates the previous value generated by the pseudorandom number generator. It also saves the state of the random function in order to enable multiple execution of random numbers.

The generated random is not secure; you can make the random numbers generated secure by implementing a cryptography to securely generate pseudorandom numbers. This helps in making your data more secure and prevent any unauthorized access to data.

We also discussed how to retrieve the current system state and how to restore the previous system status using *getstate ()* and *setstate ()*, respectively. These functions determine the current internal state of a random number generator, and this information is very important when generating a sequence of data. With a program example, we saw how to record the current internal state of a random number as well as restore the internal state to its previous state using *random.setstate ()*.

We are also able to generate Numpy.random numbers using arrays and random numbers using unique IDs.

The date and time module helps in determining the date and time of the day. The date time module has various functions with a wide range of information on the date object. From the date and time module, we are able to define a datetime class inside the datetime module, and then use the *now()* function to create an object with the current date and time.

The Python module keeps track of date and time in different ways. The datetime module keeps track of the dates and time as well as converting the dates formats.

The datetime module allow you to manipulate the date and time using the date class, a timestamp and using the time class. Other methods used in date manipulation include the datetime class, *strftime()* to format date objects into string, and *strptime()* to change the datetime format. The method creates a datetime object from the date and time string.

Timedelta objects are used to predict past and future dates. A timedelta object calculates the past and future dates but doesn't print the date or time. You can also work with different time zones in your program by calling the PytZ module. Time module is also very important when working with time in Python programs. The time module enables us to determine the number of days elapsed since the epoch era.

Python manages time in floating point numbers (seconds). From our discussion, you can use the time module to determine the number of seconds elapsed since epoch era. You can also determine the current date and time based on specific format. Time can be represented based on your physical location and it's called local time. The concept of time representation forms time zone.

A time zone allows us to conform to specific standardized time within our religion and it is defined using the Coordinated Universal Time, UTC. UTC is a standard for synchronizing and coordinating the world's time.

Python time can also be represented using data structures like tuples. We are able to discuss with examples how you can use tuples to represent time. You are also able to learn how to use Python time as an object with an example, how to convert time from seconds to objects, and how to convert local time to string.

File processing is another important feature in Python programming. In this chapter, you learned about various components of a file, how to use the file path to determine the file storage location, and about various file operation processes.

You learned how to open a Python program and use various file operation modes to manipulate a file. You can open buffered binary files the same way you open the normal files for manipulation, except that the file object either returns a BufferedReader or BufferedWriter. You also learned how to close files and free up memory resources.

When writing to a file, you can use 'w' when writing a character at a time or *write()* when writing a string or block of statements. Similarly, the 'r' mode is used in reading a single character in a file while the *read()* reads a string of statements. You can specify the number of characters you need to access by modifying the read function with *read (size)*.

File I/O operations provide you with built-in functions to manipulate files in Python. The file I/O operations are classified into text I/O, binary I/O, and raw I/O. Each of these categories has a concrete object or stream. And each of the stream objects can either be a read-only, write-only, or read-write option.

A text I/O stream sends and receives string objects while a binary I/O stream accepts bytes-like objects and generates byte objects applied on non-text data. Raw I/O is a low-level building block for both binary and text streams.

The Python Print function is used to display output data on a standard output device like a display unit or printer.

Python also allows you to import the os and OS.Path modules, which have a wide range of functions to handle file operations and perform other functions of an operating system. The os module can allow you to create a directory, rename or remove directory among other functions.

Sometimes, when making a call to an unavailable or invalid file, an error message is generated. This error message can be handled by exceptions. An exception is any interruption of the normal program flow caused by a certain condition or error. Whenever an error occurs, an exception is thrown to catch the error. If the error is not handled immediately, it will result in the termination or exit of the program.

Exceptions can occur due to various errors as discussed, and by knowing what kind of error you may expect in your program, you can easily raise an exception. Exceptions can also be handled using the try...except statements, else clauses, or try..finally clauses. When exceptions occur, they affect the flow control of the program and the control is taken to the exception block before resuming the normal execution of the program. We are also able to discuss different exception classes and how each class hierarchy is applied.

Images and graphics are essential in today's data driven world. A lot of modern applications rely on the use of images and graphics to pass information. Python provides a variety of libraries you can use to process images as well as manipulate image information.

There are various computer image processing algorithms that accepts image inputs and process these inputs to meaningful information.

To use images in Python, you have to install standard library packages designed to handle image processing. Some of the common image processing Python libraries include: OpenCV, scikit, Numpy, Scipy, and the Python Imaging Library.

Based on your image processing needs, you can install the appropriate package. In this chapter, we installed pil to handle various image manipulation techniques

Graphics is an important tool in Python programming when dealing with events. Importing the graphics library allows you to draw various images and manipulate graphic images as well as change the image color and type. You also saw how to use GUI features to carry out various tasks.

The graphical user interface provides you with onscreen widgets you can interact with to create events. These events may result from either using labels to enter text, using textboxes, clicking command buttons, using list boxes, and menus.

When handling event driven programs, you can import Python modules like Tkinter and Asyncio that allow you to perform various tasks.

In our last chapter, we are able to learn about network and client/server programming using sockets. A Python program is able to provide a network access through both low level and high level network access. The lower level access provides you with basic support to socket programming as well as allow you to implement both client and server network connections.

Socket programming acts as the network backbone for communication. It makes the transfer of information between different devices and platforms possible. Sockets in Python programming are designed for sending and receiving data between various devices, with each socket having an IP address and a port number.

The socket module provides various classes to handle connections between the devices and other programs. The various classes handle the transport layer and an interface for connecting devices.

To use the socket, you have to import it to your Python program using *socket.socket()*. This allows you to import the library functions and ports used in creating client/server models and ensures that connecting devices are able to establish communication.

You are able to connect to the server machine, access a website, and also connect to a client device and execute client server programs. We were also able to discuss how communication takes place between the client and server.

You learned how Python socket programming allows you to transfer objects through the pickle method. You also now know the reasons why you should use sockets to send data and better understand how some application programs like WhatsApp, Facebook, and Twitter rely on sockets to exchange data.

You also know how information is exchanged between your device (mobile phone or computer) and the application program through CGI programming and how communication takes place.

REFERENCES

Image Credit: edureka.co

Image Credit: w3schools.com

Image Credit: tutorialspoint.com

Image Credit: realPython.com

https://python-textbok.readthedocs.io/en/1.0/Introduction.html

https://developers.google.com/edu/python/strings

https://www.tutorialspoint.com/python/python_strings.htm

https://data-flair.training/blogs/python-sequence/

https://docs.python.org/2/library/sets.html

https://data-flair.training/blogs/python-set-and-booleans-with-examples/

https://en.wikibooks.org/wiki/Python_Programming/Sequences

https://www.geeksforgeeks.org/python-dictionary/

https://www.tutorialsteacher.com/python/math-module

https://realpython.com/python-random/

https://www.tutorialsteacher.com/python/random-module

https://www.geeksforgeeks.org/random-seed-in-python/

https://pynative.com/python-random-module/

https://www.programiz.com/python-programming/datetime

https://www.tutorialspoint.com/python/python_date_time.htm

https://www.programiz.com/python-programming/time

https://realpython.com/python-time-module/

https://www.programiz.com/python-programming/file-operation

https://docs.python.org/3/library/io.html

https://www.edureka.co/blog/os-module-in-python

https://www.geeksforgeeks.org/os-path-module-python/

https://docs.python.org/3/library/exceptions.html

http://www.co-pylit.org/courses/cosc1336/simple-graphics/01-python-graphics.html

https://www.tutorialspoint.com/concurrency_in_python/concurrency_in_python_eventdriven_programming.htm

https://www.edureka.co/blog/socket-programming-python/

https://realpython.com/python-sockets/

Printed in Great Britain
by Amazon

17985269R00115